tj

Most grateful,

Touch
Mooning Lon Chaney
How to Roast a Pepper
Gift of the Spice People

Four Plays

duck's breath books
Woodstock, NY

Four Plays
by ty adams

Published in the United States by duck's breath books, P.O. Box 1256, Woodstock, New York.

ISBN: 978-0-615-23750-3

Cover design by Ingrid Buuck
Front cover images of pottery created by
Natacha Atelier Fidler

Printed in the United States of America

ACKNOWLEDGMENT

Ty Adams wishes to thank Paul Cooper for his knowledge and patience in the publishing of this book.

to ingrid with all my love

Introduction by Lanford Wilson
Pulitzer Prize-winning playwright
and founder of the Circle Repertory Theatre, NYC

Many friends who visited New York City for their annual theater tours have told me some of their most enjoyable evenings were spent at the Circle Rep Lab: A place where scripts were presented with sometimes minimal sets but unusually fine productions, with actors from the best company I've known. Also the plays were written by some of the best young writers in the city. One of the bright and shining stars at our Lab was Ty Adams.

What a great pleasure is it to see his work finally published – where we can all read and study his sometimes screwy and always pertinent, always different, always excellent plays at our leisure. Maybe, finally getting a chance to study his work, I can find how the hell he does that.

You will enjoy this collection.

Lanford Wilson

How to Roast a Pepper

ty adams

How to Roast a Pepper was first presented November 8, 1996 by The Lab Theater Company in Residence at the West Bank in New York City with the following cast:

Delores Pink Dove	Cyndi Coyne
Grady "Catfish" Dove	Mark Shannon

Directed by Kelly Kimball

How to Roast a Pepper

Characters

Delores Pink Dove: thirties.

Grady "Catfish" Dove: forties.

Place: A trailer park. Rural Mississippi.

Time: Now.

Set

A cheap plastic lounge chair, a small cooler.

An inexpensive outdoor grill with side table.

Optional

If the budget permits and the set designer is so inclined, the end of a mobile home juts out from stage right revealing the doorway to the trailer.

Ext. Trailer Park

Music. ZZ Top's "Blue Jean Blues". The trailer park is halfway between Hattiesburg and Biloxi, Mississipi; halfway between nowhere in any direction.

On a cheap, outdoor lounge chair is stretched Grady Dove. He quietly nurses a hangover. He is dressed in blue jeans, t-shirt and boots. He is a solid, well built man, a byproduct of five years in the prison weight room. Beside his lounge chair is a small cooler full of iced Bud.

Near the trailer entrance is a cheap, round grill on three legs; charcoal is burning, red hot and waiting.

Music crossfades:

We hear ZZ-Top's "La Grange."

Enter Delores Pink. Sweeping and flowing from the trailer as a debutante at the ball, she is crisply dressed, but on a Wal-Mart Budget; nevertheless, she floats to the music. She cradles a platter of red peppers, a marinade and brush. A cookbook. She is enjoying this cooking experience.

However, her dress and manner cannot hide the look of a woman who has weathered a lot of life in a short time; this look is accentuated by an ugly, deep, worm-shaped scar that begins slightly above her right eye and travels downward, exiting below the eye. This scar she now wears proudly. Music continues as Delores goes through the ritual, by the numbers, of placing the peppers with the marinade. Music down as Grady reaches into the cooler for fresh cool buds for his eyes.

Delores: Well, look what the cat drug up.

Grady: Why weren't you there yesterday to meet me?

Delores: Your brother picked you up didn't he?

Grady: My brother's not my wife.

Delores: He'll be glad to hear that.

Grady: What is that shit on the grill?

Delores: Roasted red peppers.

How to Roast a Pepper

Grady: I'm not eatin' that shit.

(Delores tends to her peppers.)

Grady: I didn't spend five years in prison eatin' garbage to come home an' eat rabbit food.

Delores: How's the hangover?

Grady: Don't worry about it. I can hold my liquor.

Delores: That's your problem Grady; you can hold too much liquor.

Grady: I don't need you to tell me; my own wife.

Delores: You get outa prison, get drunk and stay out all night; that looks real good Grady.

Grady: I was celebratin'.

Delores: At Igor's?   That's like celebratin' at the morgue.

Grady: We don't know that now do we Delores?

Delores: I know that; I've been to Igor's; I've got a scar to prove it.

Grady: Don't be bringin' that up.

Delores: What else do we have to talk about Grady?

Grady: Why weren't you there yesterday? I walked outa prison lookin' for my wife. Where were you Delores?

Delores: My counselor said...

Grady: *(mocking)* "My counselor said..."

Delores: For two years Grady, I tried to visit you; I tried to talk to you; that visitor's room was a joke; you wouldn't talk in front of all those people; 'member? I tried.

Grady: Why aren't you wearin' your eye patch?

Delores: My counselor said I should be proud of my scar. It's my badge of courage.

Grady: You're gonna wear the patch.

Delores: Get use to it Grady.

Grady: You're gonna wear the patch god damnit.

Delores: Why should I?

Grady: It's ugly.

Delores: Thank you Grady.

Grady: I'm not gonna be seen with ya.

Delores: Not gonna be seen with me? You're the x-con.

Grady: You're wearin' the patch. That's it.

Delores: Oh that's real pretty; a black patch across my face; lovely.

Grady: Whatever, whatever happened to plastic surgery? 'member? "I gotta have so much money Grady." "Plastic surgery Grady..."

How to Roast a Pepper

Delores: I had no medical...

Grady: "Gimme the money Grady." I had my brother sell two of my catfish ponds, Delores, whatever happened to "Plastic Surgery"?

Delores: I had no medical insurance Grady. The surgery was thirty thousand...

Grady: Don't cost no fuckin'...

Delores: Thirty thousand dollars. And yes, you sold two of your catfish ponds for me.

Grady: Worked all my life to build that business.

Delores: You still have three ponds; stop moanin'; half the restaurants in Biloxi still buy your catfish. Your brother's done a good job.

Grady: So where's my money?

Delores: In the bank Grady. Haven't touched it.

Grady: That's because it's not yours to touch.

Delores: It wasn't enough money for the surgery but that was for the better; I'm proud of my scar.

Grady: You be proud Delores.

Delores: Five years. I've been busy Grady...

Grady: I'll bet you have.

Delores: Busy buildin' myself. Studyin'. I can cook now.

Grady: You call that cookin'?

Delores: I can, I can cook and I can work. You wanted me home. Cleanin' all the time. 'Member?

Grady: Filthy house; I 'member.

Delores: I have a job now.

Grady: What? Washin' old ladies hair at the beauty parlor?

Delores: Self esteem Grady. I have it. You don't.

Grady: And what's this shit I hear 'bout you takin' your maiden name back?

Delores: Who told you that?

Grady: Never mind who...when you married me, Delores, you took My Name. Now that's traditional. Nothin' wrong with that.

Delores: <u>Delores</u> <u>Pink</u> <u>Dove.</u> You're right. Nothin' wrong with that.

Grady: I gave you that name.

Delores: It's, it's, it's nothin' personal Grady.

Grady: It is personal. It's my name. I gave it to you.

Delores: Delores Pink Dove. It's like I belong on a reservation or somethin'.

How to Roast a Pepper

Grady: You didn't mind it when I married ya.

Delores: I was fifteen.

Grady: So?

Delores: So when you're fifteen you'll meet anybody at the ferris wheel.

Grady: Well I'm still your husband and I'm tellin' ya, you're a Dove. You married a Dove. If you had kids, they'd be Doves. And their kids would be grand-Doves and a Dove don't eat that shit. Now I want a steak, a baked potato with real butter, and a cold beer and a wife with my last name. I want it Delores <u>Dove.</u>

Delores: You can want it Grady.

Grady: I'm gonna get it.

Delores: Nothin' wrong with wantin' things.

Grady: Rare, I like my meat rare...

Delores: I like roasted red...

Grady: I want it Delores.

Delores: Okay, let's see...

> *(Delores studies her cook book. Thumbs pages.)*

Delores: Rare? Rare? Rare steak? I don't see it in here Grady.

Grady: Put the book down Delores.

Delores: I like my book.

Grady: Put the book down and walk away.

Delores: I <u>do</u> <u>see</u> roasted red peppers, marinated in virgin olive oil...

Grady: I wanna steak.

Delores: With just a hint of garlic.

Grady: Steak goddamn it!

Delores: Don't see it.

Grady: You're pushin' me goddamnit.

Delores: Pushin' you?

Grady: You're doin' it.

Delores: Why would I push you Grady?

Grady: You want me to pay. Well I've paid goddamnit. I went to prison for an accident.

Delores: An accident? *(pause)* An accident Grady?

Grady: They happen everyday.

Delores: Are you tryin' to say...?

Grady: Accidents happen.

Delores: You're the victim?

How to Roast a Pepper

Grady: You didn't go to prison.

Delores: You put a bullet in my head Grady. I'm carryin' it now, as we speak.

Grady: Wasn't my fault.

Delores: A bullet this close to my brain.

Grady: Huh, what brain?

Delores: The doctors opened me up; took one look. Wouldn't touch it. Too close. Too risky. I'm stuck with it. It's my payload Grady. My baggage; starts throbbin' with the slightest temperature change; every noise that enters my ear is a thousand times normal; every foot of water I try to swim...you know I use to love to swim. I've had to give that up; somethin' I loved...give it up. Water pressure; it's too much pain; so you might have to share that "victim" thing with me.

(Delores bastes her peppers. Grady nurses his eyes)

Grady: I gave you that little handgun for protection goddamnit. You asked me...

Delores: I did ask.

Grady: And I got it.

Delores: You did.

Grady: Well it, it, it seems to me it's a, it's a, a, a...

Delores: Irony?

Grady: I know what it is.

Delores: What is it Grady?

Grady: It's a fuckin' irony that's what it is.

Delores: It is ironic, I guess, you gave me a gun for protection, and you wound up shootin' me with it.

Grady: You shouldn't've interfered.

Delores: My husband was beatin' a man to death...

Grady: Is he dead? Is he? Hell no.

Delores: The man's, the man's crime was askin' me to dance.

Grady: The man...I'll tellya the man's crime Delores; the man's crime was puttin' his hands all over my wife's ass; that was his crime; what, what, what kind of dancin' is that? Huh? What kind Delores? This is Mississippi; Mississippi goddamnit. Not fuckin' Sao Paulo Brazil or somewhere. We're not doin' the Lombado here.

Delores: *(a glance to her watch)* Turn peppers.

> *(She tends to the peppers. Turns them, bastes them gently.)*

Grady: His, his, his crime was playin' with my wife's ass.

Delores: You were shootin' pool, whadayou know.

How to Roast a Pepper

Grady: I know what I saw.

Delores: You and your buddies, for hours, shootin' pool.

Grady: It's a thinkin' man's game Delores.

Delores: Shootin' pool?

Grady: It takes time...

Delores: What am I gonna do all this time? What? Watch these "thinkin' men" push a ball around a table? I didn't drink. I didn't smoke. I <u>danced</u>...and to this day what angers me the most is... I asked you for permission.

Grady: And what's wrong with that?

Delores: Permission to dance?

Grady: What?

Delores: I'm a grown woman Grady.

Grady: You're my fuckin' wife.

Delores: And a grown woman.

Grady: With a fine ass that, I suppose, any guy who wants to dance, can play with? Is that...?

Delores: Yes.

Grady: Not my wife.

Delores: My counselor said...

Grady: What-the-fuck does she know?

Delores: <u>He.</u>

Grady: What tha fuck does that fag know?

Delores: He has helped me with my self-esteem Grady. I can decide when I want to dance and who touches my ass.

Grady: That ass-grabber's lucky.

Delores: Oh I don't think so; you destroyed his face.

Grady: Lucky I didn't kill 'im.

Delores: No, he wasn't lucky Grady; you beat him beyond...he doesn't have any teeth... his nose...his jaw...you almost bit his ear off.

Grady: I oughta charge him a fee for makin' him better lookin'.

Delores: And if you hadn't been drinkin', losin' your temper and beatin' up on fellas in bars for the past 20 years on a regular basis then the judge might've seen it different but...

Grady: I don't start 'em.

Delores: But you know how to finish 'em don'tcha?

Grady: Damn right.

Delores: Strong man.

Grady: Survival.

How to Roast a Pepper

Delores: That's what it's all about. Right?

Grady: You know it.

Delores: I do know it.

Grady: I'm the one who went to prison Delores; what do you know about survival?

Delores: I survived you.

Grady: I didn't come up behind you and hit you over the head with a gun, so don't...

Delores: Don't what?

Grady: Don't....how stupid are you Delores? Look it up. Anywhere. <u>Look</u> it <u>up</u>. Never, never come up behind two men fightin'; two men in the heat of battle. Rule number one. I hate to say it, I hate to say it but....you deserve whatcha get. Look it up.

Delores: And what book do I look that up in Grady?

(Grady points to Delores's cook book)

Grady: Right there. Look it up.

(Delores grabs her book.)

Delores: Let's see, let's see... *(turns pages)* two men fightin', two men fightin', two men fightin', don't see it.

Grady: Who had the gun? Who had the gun Delores?

Delores: That's, that's not...

Grady: <u>You</u> had the gun.

Delores: But that's not what happened is it Grady?

Grady: You could've killed us both.

Delores: Let's talk about what happened.

Grady: A man doesn't know...

Delores: I've been waitin' five long years...

Grady: Well I haven't been at no country club.

Delores: What happened Grady?

Grady: All I knew was...somebody hit me from behind.   I reacted.

Delores: You took the gun away from me so fast.

Grady: You could've been anybody.

Delores: But I wasn't...

Grady: Anybody...

Delores: Too many beers right Grady.

Grady: I'd been drinkin' a little...

Delores: What else?

Grady: Can't shoot pool without a shot of tequila.

Delores: Thinkin' man's game. Right?

Grady: That's right.

Delores: "A shot of ta-kill-ya."

Grady: It was dark too...anything can happen in a bar in the dark.

Delores: And it did. To me.

Grady: Well there's a lesson Delores; stay outa bars.

Delores: But, but, but something else happened. After you took the gun from me; for a moment, for a brief...for tha, tha, tha flick of a humming bird's wing, it was that brief...

Grady: What?

Delores: We looked at each other.

Grady: That's bullshit.

Delores: We actually looked into each other's eyes.

Grady: I didn't know who it was.

Delores: We looked. The earth stopped. We looked Grady.

Grady: You've been breathin' that charcoal too long.

Delores: No, I've been relivin' that moment for five years Grady. You looked at me, and I looked at you; it stands out 'cause it was so rare; sort of like the way we looked at each other on the ferris wheel way back when. All motion ceased and husband and wife were on the floor, eye-to-eye, then....<u>you</u> <u>shot</u> <u>me</u>.

Grady: You're crazy.

Delores: You knew.

Grady: Bullshit.

Delores: You knew who you were shootin'.

Grady: You got brain damage Delores.

Delores: I got a piece of floating glass for an eye. That's what I got Grady. See?   You haven't really seen it 'cause you like the patch.   Maybe you need to see it; it looks just like my other eye; they did a good job don'tcha think? Matchin'?

Grady: I've had enough of this.

Delores: Why did you shoot me Grady?

Grady: Stop pushin' me.

Delores: What did I ever do to you?

Grady: Stop pushin' me.

Delores: Why did you shoot me?

Grady: I've paid goddamnit. Five years in that rathole; a lot of time to do a lot of thinkin'. I've talked with counselors; I've gone without sleep; I've searched and I've searched and I've searched.

How to Roast a Pepper

Delores: And what did you come up with?

Grady: It was an accident.

Delores: That the best you can do Grady?

Grady : It's the best.

Delores: It's not good enough.

> *(Grady explodes; kicking the lounge chair.)*

Grady: It's good enough...and I'll tell ya why it's good enough.

> *(Grady walks slowly to Delores. Close to her side.)*

Grady: <u>Why</u> <u>are</u> <u>you</u> <u>still</u> <u>here?</u> Sixty-four thousand dollar question. I'll answer it for ya Delores; you're still here cause you need old Grady Dove; the dove-man, your-love-man; you're here, you're here cause old Grady'll take you. Not many men. Not many men want a woman with a "glass eye." And a scar so ugly it'll make a maggot gag. Old gimp eyed-pink-woman. Slightly used black patch included. But Grady'll take you. You knew that. That's why you're here. Now I'm goin' in to <u>my</u> home and rest <u>my</u> eyes on <u>my</u> sofa... Call me when <u>my</u> steak is ready.

> *(Grady exits into trailer. Delores stares ahead. She is clearly shaken.)*

Grady: *(OS)* Delores Pink Dove? I want two cold beers for my tired eyes.

ty adams

(Delores stares.)

Grady: Did you hear me?

(Delores looks to the cooler.)

Grady: Don't make me come out there.

(Delores walks to the cooler.)

Grady: Where's my beer goddamnit?

(Delores reaches in for the two beers. Pauses. Goes back to the grill. Puts on her cooking mittens. She picks up two hot roasted peppers. Walks to the open trailer door, exits.)

end of play

Gift of the Spice People

ty adams

Gift of the Spice People was first presented by Circle Rep Lab (Michael Warren Powell, Artistic Director), New York City, in 1991 with the following cast:

Lars Kendall	Jim Abele
Cybele Browning	Johanna Day
Daniel Zupek	Stewart Clarke
Dad	Stuart Rudin

Gift of the Spice People

Characters

Lars Kendall	Late thirties, aging hippie, long hair, tired look.
Cybele Browning	Thirties, attractive, outdoorsy. Keeper of the big cats, Audubon Zoo.
Daniel Zupek	Twenties, Assistant Director of the Visual Arts Center, New Orleans. Yuppie.
Dad:	An elderly man of frail statue; the father of Lars and Daniel.
Scene:	There are three playing areas:
	Stage left – A bedroom, Lars' home. A small cot or single bed, and telephone. A large crate center stage changes roles with each playing area. In the home, the crate serves as a desk. There is a bathtub downstage between the desk and the audience.
	Center stage – Audubon Zoo. The large wooden crate holds an animal, yet to be processed. Further stage right, a large rock with stripes created by shadows from

trees. These stripes should be simulated with lighting or simply imagined. A shower/curtain effect can be used to conceal the bed.

Stage right – The Visual Arts Center. The rock becomes a sculpture. It has a light blue, weathered effect, covered with dark stripes. A telephone appears on the floor. The large wooden crate is unpacked art for a future show. The bathtub can also be a piece of sculpture. The concept of set design is one space with the three playing areas coming to life within that one set space.

Time:	The present.
Place:	New Orleans.

Gift of the Spice People

SCENE I *The sound of a pan flute; haunting music as a silhouette appears; Lars holding his dad; facing the audience; eventually he walks to the bathtub; gently places his dad in tub; music down; water splashing. Lights up on Lars giving his dad a bath. Dad stares into blank space. Lars gently bathes his dad. Lars's towel rests on his shoulder.*

Lars: The lines in your face are deeper now. When I was little I asked you about those lines. You said, "I walked into a spider's web and didn't wipe it off." I believed you. *(pause)* Funny...

I was about ten then, wasn't I? Yeah, ten. Cause I remember going to the docks for the first time. You were getting off work. You and your buddies, a bunch of hardhats jumpin' out of a Shell Oil helicopter. You put your hardhat on me; I liked that, then went to get your paycheck. I waited, facing the river, a kid on a crate of bananas. Knockin' my heels against the crate!

You didn't tell me about the spiders in the crates Dad; thanks a lot. It must've crawled up my leg or maybe from behind me. Up my shirt. Down my neck. Doesn't matter, it-got-there. I felt a stinging in my chest. Ten-year-old-arms hitting my chest, tearing at my shirt. You found me crying, sitting on the dock. A red spot on my chest. A spider from the Banana Republic and I must've upset it with my heels on the crate. We walked home and you opened my shirt.

25

Lars: Purple, swollen chest. I was dying. I was convinced I was dying. HISTORY AT TEN.

You took a mouthful of chewing tobacco, rubbed it into my chest and said, "Spider's spin silk of purple and fill the chests of special people. ONLY special people. Any kid with a purple chest was special and couldn't die."

I believed you. I was pissed off a week later when my chest turned to a normal color, remember that?

(Lars lifts his father. He walks to the bed.)

You know I think you're gainin' weight. You gain weight on me and I'll have to get one of those dollies, you know, dollies?...movin' vans?

(Lars tucks him into the bed. Picks up a catheter from side of bed. Examines it.)

Your catheter is broken. Not a good time Dad. I, I can't believe it. I just bought it. Well, I can always pick up some quick money at that bar upstairs at Commander's Palace; two drinks, all you have to know; Ramos Gin Fizz, Brandy Milk Punches... tourist drinks,.....what am I thinking? I'd go crazy.

(Removes his watch.)

Introducing...Rolex Catheters! Why not. Quick money, no tourists. Should be able to get a little cash for this; I'll get you a new diabetic joke while I'm there; 'member that last diabetic joke?

Gift of the Spice People

(Dad attempts to speak)

Lars: What? You wanna talk? Now you wanna talk? You sit in the bath and say nothing and...okay.

(Lars leans closer, pulls away quickly.)

DON'T YELL AT ME. You used to do that to me. I'd whisper something and you'd, you'd go, "DON'T YELL AT ME." And I'd laugh...that was a pretty stupid joke Dad.

(Dad attempts to speak.)

What? What is it?

(Lars leans closer.)

Daniel? Daniel? Is that what 'ya...no it's me Dad; ME, LARS. I just gave you a...Daniel isn't here; he's, he's working. He'll come by later. It's just that uh, well it's; that's the way it is. It's me. Please remember it's me. It's me Dad. Lars? The Bath? Remember? Everyday, I give you; everyday...and, and change your sheets; you like clean sheets, 'member?

Damn it....where are you Daniel?

(Daniel appears in a spot stage right.)

Daniel: Over here.

SCENE II *The Visual Arts Center, New Orleans. Lars joins Daniel observing a large rock. The rock is a sculpture.*

Daniel: It's a stunning piece of work, don't you think?

Lars: Stunning.

Daniel: Almost paleolithic in its feeling of time, yes?

Lars: Almost.

Daniel: I particularly like the individual elements of this work. More fragmented, ordinary and disparate than his earlier works, and at times more referential. Have you noticed?

In his earlier works...

Lars: Daniel...I, I, I can't do this anymore.

Daniel: Do what?

Lars: This is a rock.

Daniel: It has evolved.

Lars: I know that but...

Daniel: Think evolution forchrissake.

Lars: Evolution?

Daniel: Evolution.

Lars: Okay. In the beginning there was nothing but rock.

Daniel: Well, in the VERY beginning...

Lars: Then someone invented the wheel...

Daniel: That came much later.

Gift of the Spice People

Lars: Then everything began to roll.

Daniel: Don't say it...

Lars: Rock and roll...It's a joke.

Daniel: Bad joke. Listen Lars, this man, this, this genius...

Lars: Does he sign his work?

Daniel: That's so gauche.

Lars: Well, some people sign their work.

Daniel: Bernard LeBlanc is not some people; a brilliant young Haitian; he has curiosity deeper than an abyss; a curiosity that permeates the very skin on the word ROCK. For our last show he did a series of these plus figurines and assorted objets d'art... He calls this one "Jailhouse Rock."

Lars: Sounds familiar. Didn't Elvis...?

Daniel: *(interrupts)* His discovery of the dual possibilities of line as unbridled feelings and as legible sign is especially apparent in the parallel configurations of the jail bars. Why are you here Lars?

Lars: You said you could spare ten minutes.

Daniel: *(glances at watch)* That was seven minutes ago. Why are you...?

Lars: I thought I'd get involved; you know, do something, something creative.

Daniel: Creative?

Lars: A film maybe.

Daniel: A film?

Lars: You DO films?

Daniel: We DO occasionally if it's not political rhetoric, poetry, or shamanic outpouring, yes.

Lars: Good. I see...I SEE...Exterior Day. Sweltering heat. Canal Street. Overhead... The Fuji Blimp is, is doing what blimps do. Cut tothousands of people darting in the street; it could be lunch, it could be rush hour, could be the hour before lunch; could be rushing to see the blimp, just rushing. Cut tofrenzied ants darting around in harmony sort of a busy day-at-the-anthill so to speak. Cut to the people, the ants, the people, back and forth until they are indistinguishable in their rushing misery. Dolly back, revealing the Fuji Blimp again, hovering over this chaos, symbolizing the only escape there is...Dissolve to the face of the pilot, tears streaming down his face as he watches this, this confused mass of humanity; the co-pilot playing Russian roulette as the blimp staggers embarrassingly past the Kodak ad on the Superdome...the end.

(Daniel glances at his watch; begins to speak.)

Lars: Now, voice overs: I was thinking of a highly visible person to narrate, you know, a newscaster, weatherperson, a respected voice like, like, like...

30

Gift of the Spice People

Daniel: Jacques Cousteau?

Lars: Jacques Cousteau.

Daniel: He's dead.

Lars: Perfect. This is New Orleans; they'll love that.

Daniel: Hopeless.

Lars: But wouldn't it be more visually powerful if we just had beautiful, well-paced classical music...

Daniel: *(Glances at watch)* Thirty seconds.

Lars: Classical music as an audio over this, this chaos we're experiencing, sort of, sort of a...

Daniel: Kurasawa?

Lars: Kurasawa. That's it. That's.....whadaya think?

Daniel: I think Kurasawa would faint.

Lars: Okay...

Daniel: Pass out.

Lars: That's good. That's a good reaction.

Daniel: Doesn't matter, he's dead too; Lars, what do you know about filmmaking?

Lars: More than you think... I was in a Japanese documentary filming in the quarter.

Daniel: And what role did you play?

Lars: I was...Man-in-Bar.

Daniel: You were Extra-in-Bar weren't you?

Lars: Man-in-Bar...standing closest to the camera; that means a lot.

Daniel: That also meant a lot to the 20,000 extras in Ben Hur. Times up.

(Daniel walks away.)

Lars: The Japanese documentary was about an American poet, originally from New Orleans, but he lived in Japan most of his life. In Japan he was famous and respected but in his hometown, he was nothing.

Daniel: Time's up.

Lars: He had to go to Japan to be something.

Daniel: So do a lot of fish.

Lars: But this idea, the ants, Kurasawa...

Daniel: "Ideas are like rabbits. You get a couple and pretty soon you have a dozen."...John Steinbeck.

Lars: I think I'll stick with the ants.

Gift of the Spice People

Daniel: Suggestion: Take an intro-to-film class at Tulane, take it again, again, and again, then move to California, I'm busy.

(Daniel walks away, checks inside the crate.)

Lars: How much do you pay people to work here; you know, labor? Opening crates?

Daniel: We only use student volunteers. Tight budget.

Lars: So if I took that class at Tulane I'd qualify as a student volunteer?

Daniel: How old are you?

Lars: Thirty-somethin'.

Daniel: That was a television show wasn't it Lars?

Lars: I don't watch television.

Daniel: You look older.

Lars: Older?

Daniel: Tired. You look tired.

Lars: I'm supposed to be thirty-seven but I was sick one year. It's a joke.

Daniel: Funny...goodbye. *(to himself)* Walk away.

(Daniel picks up a clipboard near the telephone on the floor. Studies it.)

Lars: What about my idea?

Daniel: *(to himself)* I am past walking away and am now deeply
involved in my work.

Lars: You see, the idea of the ants and the humans...

Daniel: Lars, the Visual Arts Center caters to professionals;
artists with a command of their craft. You can't just put
forth ideas, thinking they are something other than;
I mean, I mean,

> *(Daniel points to the bathtub.)*

Look at this.

> *(Lars not impressed)*

> *(Daniel looks at rock.)*

Okay...look at this. There are several old masters in Haiti.

Lars: There are several old Elvis albums in Haiti.

Daniel: You have to leave now Lars.

Lars: What about my idea?

Daniel: Public domain, everyone has an idea. Develop it.

Lars: Develop it?

Daniel: Then go, go out and sell it to someone else.

Lars: Picture this...

Gift of the Spice People

Daniel: You have to leave now Lars.

Lars: A lot of ants in a room...

(Daniel goes to the telephone.)

Daniel: I'm calling...

Lars: In another room...

Daniel: I'm calling "Security".

(Daniel begins dialing.)

Lars: A lot of people.

Daniel: *(to tele)* Suzie.

Lars: Someone delivers barbecued ribs...

Daniel: *(tapping the tele)* Suzie...?

Lars: Suzie delivers barbecued ribs...

Daniel: Suzie, do me a favor...

Lars: The ants tip Suzie.

Daniel: Walk to the front and have the Security guard report to me immediately. *(listens)* Thank you.

(Daniel hangs up.)

Lars: The humans do not tip Suzie...

Daniel: *(picks up phone)* Suzie...?

Lars: The humans, being more intelligent, begin by hoarding, then arguing and eventually fighting over who has the most barbeque.

Daniel: Suzie?

(Daniel is banging on the phone.)

Lars: Animals in complete command of their craft.

Daniel: I'm not listening.

Lars: Animals feeding on each other.

(Daniel hangs up the phone.)

Daniel: Lars, it seems you're pushing yourself to make convincing wholes out of elements that are as off-key and negligible as possible. And this may account for the confusing combination of rigor and self-indulgence, of attention and real neglect your ideas communicate to me. *(pause)* Why do we do this?

Lars: Do what?

Daniel: THIS.

Lars: Because...we're glad to see each other?

Daniel: I...I mean, you're my brother. My brother. Why do we...?

Lars: I don't know.

Daniel: There was a time, when I was...little; I actually, I wanted to be like you. You. God. Well, that was then, this is now.

Lars: And what is now Daniel?

Daniel: Work.

Lars: Is that what it is?

Daniel: It's the next phase.

Lars: The "dual possibilities of line" phase?

Daniel: You can make fun; you can...I speak that way because it's the language of my business. Business has its own language but you wouldn't know that because you have no business; no I take that back; you've been in the BAR BUSINESS for some time haven't you?

Lars: I've been LET-GO.

Daniel: But at least you have THE LANGUAGE. You can take it on with you to the next bar or, or it may come in handy at some ZZ TOP concert at Tipitinas.

Lars: ZZ Top never played Tips'.

Daniel: Well they played SOMEWHERE.

Lars: Fifty-thousand plus, Tulane Stadium.

Daniel: Go there.

Lars: They tore it down.

Daniel: Go somewhere. THIS, this is my place. My work. It's not much to you but I'm not going anywhere; I'm committed here; don't mess this up for me. Get a real job Lars. You need something real.

Lars: A real job?

Daniel: Yes.

Lars: Something that comes natural?

Daniel: Right.

Lars: Second nature?

Daniel: Wasn't it second nature for you to walk into any bar and make a hundred dollars holding a burning cigarette to your arm for five seconds.

Lars: Ten seconds.

Daniel: There's extra money. Or, or what about that time you went to the South Pacific...

Lars: Which time?

Daniel: You packed three suitcases of blue jeans...

Lars: Levi's...

Daniel: Flew to Jakarta, sold them for fifty bucks each...

Lars: Seventy-five.

Gift of the Spice People

Daniel: Then hitched across Asia without a care in the world... I wanted to be you; I wanted long hair, bell bottoms and a pair of J.C.'s...

Lars: I still have those sandles.

Daniel: Those sandles were THEN. What are you doing now?

Lars: I bathe and care for animals.

Daniel: Audubon Zoo...volunteer. *(a look to his watch)* I think they're interviewing new people right now.

Lars: Audubon Zoo, okay, let's see, I'll need a special language to go with, with that. Words, lots of words, uhhh, stench, catheter; that's two, I, I need more. Gotta have a convincing group, right Daniel. Uhhh, I[m not very good at this, uhhh, stench, catheter, shit, insulin, needles, blood...

Daniel: How is he? *(silence)* HOW IS HE?

Lars: One's like the father, one's like the mother.

Daniel: I can't help that.

Lars: How is mother?

Daniel: We keep in touch.

Lars: That's nice. Still in Colorado?

Daniel: Why are you here?

Lars: He needs a new catheter.

Daniel: What?

Lars: It wraps around the dick. It fills up with piss. It's man-made so sometimes it breaks. IT'S NECESSARY and he needs a new one.

> *(Pause. They stare.)*

Lars: CATHETER.

Daniel: He worked for Shell Oil for twenty years; what about Retirement?

Lars: That would be nice. An hourly-hard-hat-on-an-oil-rig? What retirement?

Daniel: I, I...We're on deadline.

> *(Daniel and Lars stare; Lars exits. Daniel attempts to work; can't concentrate, goes to the phone.)*

Daniel: Suzie, do me a favor; ask the Security guard to watch the second floor for me...*(pause)* an hour at the most. *(pause, he holds)* Yes? Why not? *(listens)* I'm friendly, *(listens)* That's not true; I'm usually rushing because...forget it; Suzie, will you watch...thank you.

Oh uh, you think the corner Drug would have a catheter? (pause) Catheter, it wraps around....never mind just watch the second floor.

blackout

40

Gift of the Spice People

SCENE III   *The Audubon zoo.   Atop the wooden crate with binoculars is Cybele Browning observing in the direction of the rock. Cradled in her lap is a rifle. Beside her, a clipboard w/pen. Enter Lars.*

Lars: I'm the new volunteer.

Cybele: You're late. Come on up.

Lars: What's in the crate?

Cybele: Climb.

> *(Lars climbs the crate. Sits.)*

Lars: What..?

Cybele: What?

Lars: What's in the crate?

Cybele: A spider.

> *(Lars drops to the floor.)*

Cybele: You like spiders?

Lars: I like spiders; crates, crates bother me.

Cybele: This is one of those HARMLESS CRATES; get your butt up here.

Lars: I'll wait here.

Cybele: If you wait there it'll suck the fluids out of your feet.

Lars: I'm coming up.

(Lars quickly climbs; Cybele continues to observe thru the binocs.)

Lars: Where did this spider come from?

Cybele: It's from the San Blas.

Lars: San Blas?

Cybele: Islands. Off the coast of Panama. Last summer I lived there with the Cuna Indians. They're sixteenth century you know; no coin system, no clothing, no noise, no bureaucracy.

Lars: Sounds good.

Cybele: Little Chilean steamboats unload their crates of spices and inside...

Lars: I get it.

Cybele: I think you do.

Lars: They're BIG.

Cybele: No, but they THINK big...that's another story.

(Cybele stops observing; faces Lars.)

Cybele: I'm supposed to ask you this: "Why did you volunteer to work at the zoo?" You're supposed to say something noble and heartfelt.

Gift of the Spice People

Lars: World Peace?

Cybele: Oh that's good.

(Cybele hands binoculars to Lars.)

Cybele :We're attempting to breed the spotted leopards. It's rarely done in captivity. We're gonna do it. You see the shadows on that rock? See them?

(Cybele points to the rock.)

Lars: Yeah...

Cybele: Go up about 110 degrees; he's on that ledge say about two o'clock from the uh...

Lars: Two o'clock?

Cybele: Two o'clock; you know, an angle from the rock looking down on her...you see him?

Lars: There he is.

Cybele: He's beautiful isn't he?

Lars: What's he waitin' for?

Cybele: A glance, a whiff, their favorite song, how do I know.

Lars: You're the keeper.

Cybele: They're unpredictable.

(Binoculars to Cybele, she observes.)

Lars: Why the gun?

Cybele: Tranquilizer. He could accidentally kill her during intercourse.

Lars: Kill her?

Cybele: Yep.

Lars: Rather passionate isn't he?

Cybele: He's Overkill, no pun intended.

> *(Cybele observes thru binocs.)*

Cybele: The actual mechanics of sexual climax are well known, we've studied the physiology of the sexual organs, the neurological and muscular activity during orgasm and what triggers it.

Lars: Well...?

Cybele: What?

Lars: What triggers it?

Cybele: Apparently during sexual arousal in the male prostatic and seminal fluids and semen collect in the prostatic urethra above the urethral bulb. As the pressure builds...hold it. He's moving; he's moving. Hold the gun he's moving. Quick write down the time on the daily.

> *(Lars has no watch, struggles to see her watch, looks at the sun, measures, etc.)*

Gift of the Spice People

Cybele: We'll need to record every behavioral movement and time intervals. Write this down, "Male subject stalking within twenty feet at about 90 degrees on a ledge.

(He struggles behind her back.)

Cybele: Shit. He disappeared behind some foliage.

(She looks to Lars.)

Cybele: Where was I?

Lars: The time? My watch, I must've left it...

Cybele: Uhhh, ten-forty-one.

(He writes.)

Cybele: Where was I?

(Lars reads.)

Lars: Uhhh, shit, he disappea...

(She observes thru binoculars.)

Cybele: Oh yes, as the pressure builds a point arrives when the urethral sphincter opens and the fluids rush into the urethral bulb!

(introduction) Cybele Browning, welcome aboard!

Lars: Lars Kendall.

(They shake hands.)

Cybele: If he accidentally kills her, we lose.

Lars: And if he doesn't?

Cybele: We get cubs, publicity...MONEY.

Lars: What do the animals get?

Cybele: They get...

Lars: What do the...?

Cybele: I heard you; the animals get...Well, how else would
children learn about animals? The people want what's best
for their children; the people give. The children get.

Lars: But what do the animals get?

Cybele: They get ME and I make sure they avoid extinction.

Lars: This is it!
Cybele: What?

Lars: My film.

Cybele: You're here to work.

Lars: Then you, you film it.

Cybele: Film what?

Lars: The leopards, you know, the triggers, the bulbs, the
sudden distention, everything.

Cybele: You're kidding...?

Gift of the Spice People

Lars: I'm serious.

Cybele: THAT bothers me.

Lars: The film's for the festival at the Visual Arts Center.

Cybele: I don't give a shit about festivals. This is risky work.

Lars: Risky? That's good. Adds to the drama.

Cybele: You're dealing with such a powerful animal here Lars.

Lars: But we don't get near them, touch them or anything...do we?

Cybele: I touch them.

Lars: I know but not inside...inside? You know, the cage?

Cybele: They'd kill me.

Lars: They WOULD kill you.

Cybele: The very thought of being with them can't even enter my mind.

Lars: But it does...

Cybele: I told you, it can't.

Lars: I know, you told me but...

Cybele: It can't enter my mind.

Lars: Alone, in bed at night...
Cybele: *(lying)* No...

Lars: When you think about being with them... little pebbles of flesh pop up at the nap of your neck.

(Cybele massages her neck.)

Lars: Pebbled flesh. Right there.

(Cybele quickly diverts her hand back to her work.)

Lars: Not a good title for the film though, "Pebbled Flesh." What do you think?

Cybele: Lars, look at me. I'm not going to die in the jaws of a spotted leopard just so you can make a film...understand? Anyway, who'd take care of my babies?

Lars: I would.

Cybele: No, sorry. The zoo has a network; some sadistic guy up for promotion in Atlanta would be brought in on short notice. They'd cover it up; make it look like an accident.

Lars: And the truth?

Cybele: HA. He wouldn't get near the truth.

Lars: What would they tell him?

Cybele: The last-angry-woman-from Houston committed the cardinal sin.

Lars: What's "the cardinal sin"?

Cybele: To be CLOSE to her babies.

Lars: I'd ask questions.

Cybele: They'd be suppressed.

Lars: Then I'd have someone else...

Cybele: The Curator would whitewash.

Lars: "She was competent, well-trained..."

Cybele: Deeper.

Lars: "She was competent, well-trained. She had no reason to go into the cage. We have no idea why this happened."

Cybele: Then he would TWIST....

Lars: "She jeopardized the people who had to go to her defense."

Cybele: Then he would add a little P.R.

Lars: "The two hundred full-time...

Cybele: Three hundred.

Lars: Three hundred staff members of the zoo are extremely upset..."

Cybele: HA.

Lars: "and the accidental death of this respected woman is a horrible reminder..."

Cybele: One last question...

Lars: "Sorry, it's in litigation."

Cybele: Litigation?

Lars: Your mother would sue the hell out of 'em.

Cybele: She would.

Lars: And give Me the money for Your film:

Cybele: Whoa.

Lars: "The Last Angry Woman."

Cybele: Hold it...

Lars: I like it.

Cybele: HOLD IT..."The Last Angry Woman" is still alive, here.
I'm afraid you'll have to film something else.

(Cybele looking thru binoculars.)

Lars: I thought about using ants.

Cybele: Ants?

Lars: Thousands of ants.

Cybele: Red ants? Fire ants?

Lars: Ants that like to eat.

Cybele: Forget ants.

Lars: Forget ants?

Gift of the Spice People

Cybele: Rats.

Lars: Rats?

Cybele: Rats.

Lars: But I've put so much thought into ants.

Cybele: Think about rats.

Lars: Rats...

Cybele: Rats are very similar to humans.

Lars: It's a big transition. I like ants.

Cybele: In sexual reproduction and other physiological areas, you're better off with rats.

Lars: I'm not interested in reproduction.

> *(She drops the binocs, a look.)*

Cybele: Not interested in reproduction?

Lars: No.

Cybele: *(confident)* Rats.

> *(Cybele observing again.)*

Lars: But I'm not interested in physiology.

> *(Cybele stops, a look.)*

Cybele: Not interested in physiology?

Lars: No.

Cybele: What kind of man are you?

Lars: Right now? An ant man.

Cybele: Behavior?

Lars: Right.

Cybele: Primates.

> *(Cybele observes thru binocs.)*

Lars: Primates?

Cybele: Very similar.

Lars: Primates.

> *(Cybele stops.)*

Cybele: Forget primates.

Lars: No. I want primates.

Cybele: The Keeper of the Primates is Richard Sanchez. He's knowledgeable but snoddy, technically curious but dogmatic; constantly trying to get into my pants; in short, he's a fucking asshole.

Lars: Forget primates.

Cybele: I'll think of something.

> *(Stops observing. A look.)*

Gift of the Spice People

Cybele: Let me brief you. You'll be cleaning the cages, bears, leopards, tigers. We have three Siberian tigers: Cleo, Ishtar, and Somoza, Ishtar is the white one; the two leopards are Victor and Olive; and the two bears are Nigeria and Quinn. They DO know their names or I like to think they do...so learn them. I can't disguise the work. It's three hours, every day, of shoveling wild, primal shit, with a few banana peels thrown in. The bears are responsible for the banana peels but the job is shoveling shit. Still interested?

Lars: Shit is nothing to me.

Cybele: Really? There's no salary.

Lars: That's okay.

Cybele: Hm...and when you finish the cages you'll drain and clean the sea lion's pool. The sea lions have no names but they have money. Lots of money.

Lars: I don't get it.

Cybele: Tourists. Fucking, stupid tourists. Thousands. Everyday. Nickels, dimes, quarters, baby toys, earrings and sunglasses into the sea lion's pool.

Lars: Why?

Cybele: Some warped search for good luck, who knows. My mother would say, "Gifts for Sedna, the Inuit goddess of the seals." Only Sedna doesn't care about money....it's yours.

Lars: I'm not doing this for the money.

Cybele: Keep the baby toys and throw the money away, I don't
care, just clean the pool. You're not one of those "trust
persons" are you?

Lars: You can trust me.

Cybele: Ohhh, that was...

Lars: Bad?

Cybele: Bad. But it's not that. It's <u>you</u>. There're only two types
of volunteers, believe me, I've seen them all. You're not
"Jungle Jim" and you're not "Diane Fossey".

What type are you?

Lars: O Positive.

Cybele: I'm O Positive.

Lars: You're O Positive?

Cybele: Who are you?

Lars: Nobody.

Cybele: My mother would say, "if you were somebody and you
felt like nobody you'd probably tell me you were nobody
just to throw me off.

Lars: What does your mother know?

Gift of the Spice People

Cybele: Well, she named me after the Phrygian Goddess Cybele, Guardian of the Lions.

Lars: Is it too late for her to name me?

Cybele: Who are you?

Lars: I was a Bartender.

Cybele: Oh yeah. Where?

Lars: Snug Harbor.

Cybele: Good jazz.

Lars: Fifteen years.

Cybele: Alota jazz.

Lars: Get off at 6am. Oysters-on-the-half-shell at dawn.

Cybele: Let's see: a dozen oysters a day...

Lars: Followed by a pitcher of chilled schnapps.

Lars: Three-hundred-sixty-five days a year.

Lars: Fill the sugar bowl with cocaine.

Cybele: Times fifteen years...

Lars: Then slip over to Cafe Brazil.

Cybele: I'm still working on the oysters.

Lars: They fired me.

ty *adams*

Cybele: They saved your life. God, fifteen years?

   Why did they fire you?

Lars: Stealing money.

Cybele: Did you?

Lars: No.

Cybele: You want money? You want money? Hit the sea lion
    pool! This is too good. *(she returns to looking thru binoc's)* A
    man who thinks shit is nothing! I love it.

Lars: Teach me this business.

Cybele: Hit the sea lion pool.

Lars: No, I mean...teach me.

       (She drops the binoculars. They stare.)

Lars: I need a business. I NEED SOMETHING.

Cybele: And you want this?

Lars: Yes.

       (She observes with binoculars.)

Cybele: Well, you begin with a shovel and a pile of shit.

Lars: Where did you begin?

Cybele: You ARE serious aren't you?

Lars: Yes.

Gift of the Spice People

Cybele: All you need to know: There are <u>the</u> <u>Keepers</u> <u>and</u> <u>the</u> <u>Sleepers</u> and a big gap in between.

Lars: *(writes)* "The keepers and the sleepers."

(Cybele hands him a green T-shirt.)

Cybele: Here's your volunteer T-Shirt, it'll get you through security every morning.

Lars: It's a medium.

Cybele: I'm a medium.

Lars: I'm a medium.

Cybele: It's a fit.

blackout

(Upbeat, spirited music)

SCENE IV *Next day. Visual Arts Center. Daniel enters; studies a piece of paper on the side of the crate. He writes on clipboard. Lars is standing nearby. Daniel notices.*

Daniel: How did you get in here?

(Lars is wearing his Volunteer T-shirt.)

Lars: T-shirt; gets me through security.

Daniel: This time you've gone too far.

Lars: The security guard hates your guts Daniel; I stopped and chatted for awhile; you should try it; they like that.

Daniel: He can be replaced. Now what-is-it-this-time?

Lars: Rats!

Daniel: I don't believe this.

Lars: I've decided to use rats! Rats are very much like humans and Cybele ohhh Cybele, she's wonderful. Beautiful. Intelligent. Angry. Loves animals, loves-animals. Bilingual just like you but she's more.

She's named after a goddess; she's...SHE'S A MEDIUM.

Daniel: You're crazy. I'd dial nine-one-one if I thought...

Lars: Giving up on Suzie?

Daniel: You're like that crazed woman who shot Andy Warhol. This obsession is sad Lars. We're, we're weeks away from the festival; this is, this is; you're not going to let me have this are you? You're going to fuck this up for me aren't you?

(Daniel pointing to the crate.)

There are hours of unpacking and setting up...

(Lars delivers money.)

Lars: Thanks for the catheter. Take this. It's, it's tainted with sea lion breath but it's good money.

Daniel: I don't want your money.

Gift of the Spice People

Lars: Take it.

Daniel: I don't want your money. I WANT YOU TO LEAVE.

Lars: What's in the crate?

(Lars plants the money on top.)

Daniel: None of your business...

(Lars walking around the crate, peeking inside.)

Lars: It looks empty.

Daniel: It's a minimalist piece...

Lars: It looks empty.

Daniel: TO YOU.

Lars: Well, yes...

Daniel: But to everyone else...It's full.

(Lars reads from shipment receipt taped to side of crate.)

Lars: "Bernard LeBlanc"?

Daniel: I don't have the time for this shit; we, we're in a four alarm phase here.

Lars: Let me help.

Daniel: You want to help? You want to help? Go away. Let me work. That would help. Anyway, we couldn't work together;

we can barely have a conversation. We do not click Lars; I'm not even sure we should worry about it.

Lars:: We could've been a team like, like the Wright Brothers, Neville Brothers, Blues Brothers, Uh, Dorsey Brothers...

Daniel: Dorsey Brothers?

Lars: Yeah, there was uhhh Tommy, Tommy Dorsey and...what's the other guy's name?

Daniel: You get to be him. The one nobody knows.

Lars: He asked about you.

Daniel: Tommy Dorsey?

Lars: Daniel made a joke?

Daniel: I, I...no.

Lars: I can't believe it.

Daniel: What did he say?

Lars: Well, you know Tommy; he talked about the band...

Daniel: STOP IT. What did he say?

Lars: "Daniel." Usually after he has his bath. He doesn't explain.

Daniel: You're there.

Lars: He thinks I'm you.

Daniel: Ha.

Gift of the Spice People

Lars: He's dying and he wants to see you.

Daniel: Kids do not decide. Let's get that straight. Kids do what THE COURTS decide. All I remember is moving to Colorado. And my life went by. I grew up with a father and a mother in Colorado and I can't...

Lars: How is she?

Daniel: Happy.

Lars: Happy?

Daniel: I didn't tell her you were having these, these delusions, she'd just worry.

Lars: Worry...not good.

Daniel: She calls me every week.

Lars: Does she?

Daniel: Is there anything you'd like to tell her?

Lars: (*thinks*) Tell her that I'm worried about the spotted snow leopards.

Daniel: She'll be excited to hear that.

Lars: Did you know that leopards rarely breed in captivity? Did you know that?

Daniel: A void in my life I guess.

Lars: You see, the problem seems to be language. We don't understand why they won't breed. They can't tell us. It's a problem.

Daniel : Anything else?

Lars: It's a BIG problem.

Daniel: Anything else?

Lars: Tell her....the sea lions have a lot of money.

Daniel: Fine.

Lars: Sedna, she's the one you want to touch base with.

Daniel: Why do you always push me?

(Daniel walks to phone.)

Lars: Oh no. Don't do it. Not, not,...NOT SUZIE.

Daniel: You need help Lars.

(Daniel dials the phone.)

Lars: No. I don't want help; I, I want this challenge; ALONE...just me-against-Suzie.

Daniel: *(to phone)* Hello Suzie?

Lars: A duel at dawn...

Daniel: *(to phone)* Suzie take the stairs...

Lars: With bush axes...

Daniel: Up to the vice-president's office...

Lars: In deep water, Lake Pontchartrain.

Daniel: *(to phone)* get him and come here...

Lars: How tall is Suzie?

Daniel: *(to phone)* Thank you. *(hangs up)*

Lars: If she's five-four, I want six feet of water.

Daniel: STOP IT. *(pause)*   Listen, I got the catheter...

Lars: You had it DROPPED OFF.

Daniel: I'm, I couldn't leave this; I'm stuck here; day and night; three floors of expensive... and yes, I'm kissing ass; working overtime; trying to make something of myself; what's wrong with that?

Lars: He needs to see you; he needs it so you've got to come see; JUST SEE HIM; do it for him; I don't know why; just do it.

Daniel: And you-will-not-come-back-here?

Daniel: Right.

Daniel: Fine...That's it, end of conversation.

   (Daniel exits.)

blackout

ty adams

SCENE V *Lars sits at a small desk next to the bed. The old man is in bed. Lars is counting money.*

Lars: I AM THE PERFECT MAN FOR THIS JOB! I can't believe people actually throw their money away.

(He flips a coin onto the desk.)

The Coin of the Realm! Thank you Sedna. I'll have to name the sea lions.

(He flips a coin.)

New sheets...

(He flips another coin.)

New catheter...

(From his pocket, many coins.)

In a couple of months we could buy a wheelchair, take you down by the docks, watch the dock workers; You'd like that. They've renovated the whole damn riverfront. Casinos! everybody's gone gamblin' crazy.

(Lars goes to bathtub as he speaks. Checks the water.)

Lars: Remember Benji, the dog, you know, the movie? When it first came out they said Benji got the job because he had a James Dean-like quality. Benji alone was the only dog with the right quality for the job...

Gift of the Spice People

"Fossey" type. She'll see that Olive gets processed without the usual red tape. See ya tomorrow...

(Cybele exits. Lars stares at Olive.)

Lars: My father died yesterday.

(Lars cautiously lifts the jar containing Olive; lights fade to music, preferably mystical pan flute.)

SCENE VII   *Lars at home. Sits on floor next to the phone, facing the jar. Dad remains in bed; eyes open; pale and still.*

Lars: I guess Daniel; well, you see Dad, he has this, this deadline. It's, it's important to him so give him time. Give him time.

(Lars stands, leans, examines the spider with caution. Thumps the glass; pulls away.)

(to Dad) Of course, WE don't have much time.

(to spider) Do we Olive?

(to Dad) I went by the funeral home. The best, right? That's what we want, the best. They've got everything. Wood, aluminum, plutonium...everything. Six thousand bucks.

Oh, I went by Rubensteins. A new suit? Top-of-the-line-Chevy? Three seventy-five.

Lars: The salesman took a look at me and said, "A dark suit huh? Now will that be a Rolls Royce or a top-of-the-line-

73

Gift of the Spice People

(Lars gets a towel from desk. Looks up. Speaks to the air.)

I know you Benji.

(Lars picks up father.)

Let's get that bath now.

(Lars delicately places father in the bathtub.)

Is that too cold? Too hot?

(He bathes his father.)

Times have changed Dad. Remember the old days? Bananas in-the-crate. Spider-just-along-for the ride? Well, the bananas have been demoted to bear food and, and the spiders have their own crates.

Cybele was sitting on top of one of those crates when we met. Scared the shit out of me but Cybele, Cybele makes it all sound soooo, different. This woman isn't human. She's, she's a cat, a scientist, a medium; she's worried about the leopards right now so this spider just waits... waits for "The Phrygian Goddess".

Lars: Another thing, I saw Daniel; yeah, he's comin' by; Daniel is comin' to see you; that's right. Yeah. Bout time. He's been busy. It's his work. He loves his work...that's good. He's a good kid.

Lars: Dad? Wake up now. Come on. I've got a new diabetic joke for ya. Wake up; you always look at me. Don't have to speak.   Just look at me...Dad? LOOK AT ME.

(Lars desperately lifts his father, carries him dripping to the bed.)

The, the uhh, three Siberian tigers are Cleo, Ishtar, and Somoza. Ishtar is the white one. The leopards are Victor and Olive; and, and the bears are Nigeria and Quinn.

(Lars lowers the man to the bed, begins toweling him.)

I've told you not to go to bed wet like this. How many times have I told you that? How many?

(He pulls away; fumbles desperately with a cigarette; decides not to smoke it; tears the cigarette and spreads the tobacco over the chest of his father.)

Remember this? A little tobacco on the chest, you rubbed into my chest, remember? "Spiders spin silk of purple and fill the chests of special people, only special...

(Lars gives up.)

I read the other day...   I read the other day that WILLPOWER can delay death. They did a study of a group of old Chinese women in California. The week before the Harvest Moon Festival is so important because the oldest woman in each family...are you listenin' to me? The oldest woman in each family directs the younger

66

women on how to live. At the end of the week, there's a feast where the older women are celebrated.

Lars: So they can't die that week. They DON'T DIE that week. REFUSE TO DIE that week but the week following the festival, THAT WEEK, the death rate was higher than all year. You don't even have to be Chinese, you just have to have...

> *(Lars stops. Lights fade to the sound of a pan flute.)*

SCENE VI *The next day. Audubon Zoo. Cybele stands center stage holding a small jar up to the sky. Lars enters from behind the crate pushing an empty wheelbarrow. He drops the handle.*

Lars: I fed the fish to the Sea Lions.

Cybele: That's good.

> *(She turns to face him; concealing the jar.)*

Cybele: Did you stuff the gills with vitamins?

Lars: Yeah.

Cybele: Feed the cats?

Lars: Yeah. What is that?

Cybele: Every beautiful horse that got too old to ride.

Lars: All the cats were there except Olive.

Cybele: Olive is dead.

Lars: What?

Cybele: She's dead.

Lars: She's dead?   When?

Cybele: Yesterday. I can't believe it. I mean, I was right there. I'm always there.

Lars: Always.

Cybele: It happened so quickly. I knew Victor was fast and I was ready but she ran behind the rock. Blocked my view completely; She, she has never gone behind the rock.

Lars: Never.

Cybele: And from up there I had been easily tracking both of them. Victor came down unusually fast; she moved; I lost her behind the rock; I knew I was in trouble; I dropped the binoculars, ran to the other side with the gun. He had mounted her which is expected but his claws were deep into her neck. It was too much. She was helpless. I shot him. I shot him again.

Lars: Did it put him out?

Cybele: Not quick enough. When I got to her, she was still breathing. Heavy, desperate breathing. I held her for the first time. Then her breathing slowed. Like a clock winding down. It stopped. She was gone.

After it happened I sat alone in Olive's cage. I felt MYSELF breathing, painfully conscious of my breathing. It's funny, breathing is so easy when it's unconscious but when you're feeling it, counting it, aware of it...its unbearable. I, I began noticing Olive's hair, strands of hair she left rubbing herself on the bars. I ran my hand across the bar, took her wild hair and rubbed it into my chest.

(She takes a soothing deep breath. She is relieved.)

Lars: I wish she could have run away.

Cybele: IN HERE? IN CIVILIZED SOCIETY? We think we can monitor, we think we can control; we think we're SOOO NOBLE...

Lars: These things happen...

Cybele: But on the plains...

Lars: Things die...

Cybele: On the plains of the Serengeti IF AND WHEN it happens, it happens, it's natural. We have no business holding these animals. LET THE CHILDREN LEARN THAT. You were right. You asked me, "What do the animals get?" And I, I probably said something stupid.

Lars: You said, "They get ME."

Cybele : Well, ME fucked up.

Lars: What will happen to Victor?

Cybele: Victor will remain for the pleasure of the children.

Lars: What about you?

Cybele: An Inquiry. It's already happened. This morning, early. Strange. The Curator: "Leopards are rare and cost a lot of money. Very costly Cybele, very costly. Josh, what's the market rate for a female snow leopard these days? Could run sixty to a hundred grand, wouldn't you say? We'll have to think about this Cybele." They decided I should shovel shit for awhile. They're moving you to Primates....I'm sorry about all this.

Lars: It was a stupid idea.

Cybele: What?

Lars: ME, here. The rats. The film. I, I have a weak grip on reality.

(Cybele presents the jar)

Cybele: Meet your mentor.

Lars: What's that?

Cybele: A gift.....

Lars: I, I, I... no.

Cybele: It's for me Lars.

Lars: Keep it over there; I've got this, you know this...

Gift of the Spice People

Cybele: Isn't she beautiful?

Lars: This thing.

Cybele: There's no need to be afraid.

Lars: I feel more comfortable being afraid THANK YOU.

Cybele: Olive, whadaya think? Pass the name on?

Lars: Olive is fine.

Cybele: She's traveled a long way. She doesn't know that her reputation precedes her.

Lars: Reputation? What reputation?

Cybele: Legend has it...this spider sucks juices from the bodies of dying animals but in the San Blas the only animal is the Cuna Indian. One day an old chief was dying. He was searching for a better way. No solid ground to bury the dead; no rock to build tombs of grandeur. Their only option was to bury at sea but this didn't fit into the chief's scheme of things. He was Chief! Not to be consumed by the scavengers of the sea...but preserved for posterity. So the dying day arrived and from his hammock he reached down one last time, allowing a spider to crawl up his arm. The next day, the spinnerets of silk had been layered by the Orb Weaver, golden adhesive droplets under layer after layer of golden nonadhesive silk from head to toe. Funeral garb fit for a king. And so clever. It's a natural embalming process; the chief was well-preserved because the body had been drained of all its fluids.

Lars: I don't believe it.

Cybele: Me neither.

Lars: Myth.

Cybele: I mean, we know that one spider could <u>never</u> produce enough silk to wrap a man. But one...ONE DESPERATE SPIDER who hopped off a steamboat by accident in a land with only one food source, a desperate-dying-willing-food-source, well....

Lars: Why send Olive to you?

Cybele: A gift for a gift. This wonderful little man, Cuna Indian, paddled the canoe for me; while I snorkeled, he fished, with his hands, marble hands, hands of stone; seventy years of fishing line through these hands. I mailed him a gift, a cheap Zebco rod and reel; He probably never used it; he turned it into a good-luck-charm, a God or something to worship...Zebco.

> *(She focuses on the spider.)*

Listen, tomorrow's your last day with me. Let's do something wicked. Let's put bear shit in a primate cage; fuck up Sanchez's life, whadaya say?

Lars: I don't know...

Cybele: Think about it. I'm late for a meeting. Take Olive to the insect pavilion; ask for Gloria Dupont. She's a

Chevy?" That was a joke. He laughed. I didn't.

(Lars opens a note from his pocket; reads aloud casually to himself. The Keeper and the Sleeper. He picks up the phone, dials.)

Information? I'd like the residence of Mr. Bernard LeBlanc please. Thank you. *(pause)* Uhhh, he lives in the quarter, Royal Street, I think. *(pause)* Several? Uhhh, he's an artist; probably has a studio number...I'll take it.

(Lars writes.)

Thank you.

(Lars hangs up.)

(Picks up again, dials.)

I'd like to leave a message...I'm sorry, my name is...

(Hangs up. Looks at the spider. A look to the father.)

Develop it.

(Dials phone again.)

A message for Bernard LeBlanc. After viewing your extraordinary work, the Cuna Indians feel that you are the one. Please arrange to accept a gift at 601 Rue Dauphine.

(Lars hangs up. Stares at the spider. He writes a quick note. To Bernard LeBlanc...)

Gift of the Spice People

Lars: "The Keeper and the Sleeper"

(He folds the note,, places it where it is most obvious; walks with the jar to the bed, slowly loosening the lid; he rests the jar gently on the floor. He joins Dad in bed.)

So the Chief was dying. And he decided that "a top of the line chevy" wasn't good enough. He wanted to sleep forever in a shroud of silk; slide into the nether-world where animals are treated properly.

(Lars places dad's arm under the sheets. He stretches out next to Dad, slightly higher with his back resting against a pillow. One arm goes around Dad's neck. Lars' other arm extends slowly to the floor, inviting the spider from the jar. His fear tightens his body in preparation for the spider's journey up his arm; the Lights turn a cobalt blue as a haunting pan flute fills the air. His finger flicks the lid off the jar.)

blackout

SCENE VIII *Two weeks later. Festival opening, Visual Arts Center. Jailhouse Rock" remains. A black curtain drops to cover upstage creating a more intimate feeling... Cybele, well-dressed, stands facing the rock. Daniel enters, He checks the curtain for stability. Greets several invisible guests. Notices Cybele. Approaches.*

Daniel: Nature is truly the model for everything, don't you think?

Cybele: Excuse me?

Daniel: This piece.

Cybele: Oh.

Daniel: The imagery is literally determined by nature...I'm Daniel Zupek, thank you for coming.

Cybele: Cybele Browning. I know your brother.

Daniel: Lars?

Cybele: He worked at the zoo.

Daniel: Oh yes, of course. You're the medium.

Cybele: He stopped coming, two weeks ago.

Daniel: So lucky you.

Cybele: Have you seen him?

Daniel: No.

Cybele: I read about the opening in the Picayune. I thought...

Daniel: You thought he might be here?

Cybele: Well...

Daniel: He wouldn't be here. If I were you, I wouldn't worry about it. You see, he's constantly confusing people.

Cybele: It's not that he confused me; well, he DID confuse me.

Daniel: Not surprising.

Cybele: I think he took something that belongs to me.

Daniel: Wasn't a colony of ants was it?

Cybele: No.

Daniel: Or rats? First it was a film about ants; No, no, no rats, first it was ants then rats; who knows where he got THAT idea. (pause) I hope you're not one of those people who get uptight around sculpture. They feel they need to know something about the medium to enjoy it, which isn't true. The point is to have a visceral experience, don't you think?

Cybele: The rats were my idea.

Daniel: Right. Would you, would you excuse me for just a moment? JUST, just a moment.

> *(Daniel stands aside and claps his hands. Addresses the invisible guests.)*

Daniel: EXCUSE ME. ATTENTION please. Attention. Ladies and gentlemen, the Visual Arts Center is proud to unveil the centerpiece of the collection of works by our Caribbean neighbors. This gentleman has a unique vision. Bernard LeBlanc's latest creation, he's always been attentive to titles...

> *(The black curtain drops)*

"The Keeper and the Sleeper!"

(The sculpture is a mummified bed with two men woven in golden strands of silk. The image of the sculpture should be identical to the image left us in the previous scene. The stage has darkened. The visual presence of the sculpture should be totally commanding and serene.

Daniel applauds.

Cybele begins but stops....stunned. Throughout the duration of the scene Daniel's voice and presence becomes background music as we focus upon Cybele's journey.)

Daniel: Bernard LeBlanc is a future master! His light, yet dense use of silk is a ghostly skin in which the body of nature is preserved yet absent.

His figures, no matter how old or young these men may be, they both manage to suggest tremendous pain...isn't it wonderful!

(Cybele walks slowly to the sculpture. She circles it; stops and stares at this man she recognizes, her face revealing to us her discovery.)

Daniel: Their expressions, carefully veiled with silk, not ordinary white, but golden silk, are reference points where the viewer can extract and puzzle over...wondering if they are signs of boredom, insanity, or everyday human desperation.

When I first saw this, I thought about the interior of an ancient temple in which all sorts of wonderful and terrible things took place...this piece seems alive. The circles of carefully woven silk, expanding, contrasting, as if they were trying to SCREAM.

There is a sense that these silent men hold the answer to something that is a matter of life and death....

(A spot remains on Cybele and the sculpture as she reaches out to it.)

Daniel : Miss Browning?

(She does not hear him. Lights fade with pan flute music; haunting; poignant sound.)

end of play

ty adams

Mooning Lon Chaney

Mooning Lon Chaney was first presented at The Neighborhood Playhouse in New York City, in 1998 with the following cast:

Lon Chaney III	David Arrow
Nash of the Nocturne	Mick Weber

Author's Note:

All characters mentioned in this play from Lon Chaney's childhood are fictional and bear no resemblance to the real people they are named after.

Mooning Lon Chaney

Lon Chaney III...   Man. Twenties.

Nash of the Nocturne... Man. Forties

Place: Evansville, anywhere USA.

Radio station. Disk.jockey booth.

This is AM Talk radio, located on the skirts of town. Not the biggest. Not the most successful station in town.

Time: A little before midnight.

SCENE Darkness. The Sound of a wolf howling. Crossfade into music. The music is syncopated, nocturnal, and bounding.

Two spot lights up, revealing a small radio station DJ booth.

Two men sit diagonally, Nash of the Nocturne and Lon Chaney III. Two microphones loom over them and down to their faces.

They gaze around, waiting for a commercial break to end.

Lon appears to have slept in his clothing; his hair is matted and he seems to have missed a lot of life.

Nash receives his cue…

Nash: Welcome back night people; you're listening to Nash-of-the-Nocturne shift, WADO AM 660 on your dial; blasting from the skirts of Evansville, just over Pier One, next to Motel Six. Our guest, this wee hour before midnight, claims he was swept in by the winds of destiny. Actually, he was a call-in a week ago.

I listened to his improbable story. Red flags went up, so I had our producer Stephanie, do a background. Important. I've had more than my share of psycho-ward-cutbacks; disgruntled postal workers, and loners living west of the Mississippi in a log cabin.

Our guest checked out okay so we brought him in, booked 'im first-class-Grey Hunde' Express; set 'im up next door at Motel Six; and here he is....Lon Chaney Junior.

Lon: Tha, tha third.

Nash: 'Cuse me?

Lon: Tha third.

Nash: Tha third. Sorry. Lon Chaney tha third. The grandson is it?

Lon: Right.

Nash: Grandson of the silent screen star Lon Chaney, the man of a thousand faces, zatright?

Lon: He was a nut.

Nash: Okay, "tha nut" Chaney your grandfather and his son...

Lon: Junior.

Nash: Your father, Lon Chaney Jr.; starred in that movie made back in tha fifties, whatwasit...?

Lon: THE WOLF MAN.

Nash: Right. THE WOLF MAN. Was Junior another nut?

Lon: I, I, I don't know. I never knew him.

Nash: Right. And that's why we're here aren't we Lon. To know. To get that monkey, or should I say, monster off your back. Not something you asked for; not something you deserved; not a card usually dealt a child but something ugly that grew and turned your small-minded-small-town-neighbors into vigilantes, zatright?

Lon: Fletcher Thornton.

Nash: Fletcher Thornton?

Lon: Was one of them.

Nash: Of course he was, that naughty, naughty Fletcher T.

Lon: What is that?

Nash: What?

Lon: THAT?

Nash: Music. Just music Lon.

ty adams

Lon: It's not right.

Nash: Just music...

Lon: It's not right.

Nash: My show, my show Lon; not a moral decision.

Lon: I'm telling you, It's not right.

Nash: The music is wrong?

Lon: Very wrong.

Nash: Oh that hurts Lon.

Lon: Please turn it down; Please I can't take, I CAN'T TAKE IT.

(Nash turns the music down..)

Nash: Okay okay okay. It's down. Better? What, what should it be Lon? The music. You tell us...

Lon : You don't have time. You don't have time. You think you have time but you don't. The music grabs you. First thing that goes...the nervous system. It's midnight and the nervous....ZIP. Gone.

The dark, dancing rhythms succeed in galvanizing your nervous system. Your mind, neither has the time nor the balance to sort out these queasy, quivering sounds before they become parts of your aesthetic domain. Your nerves have beaten your reason to the punch, and you find yourself, against your better wisdom casting questioning glances at the person next to you, for, like it or not neurologically, we all have been programmed for flight... the music is all wrong.

Nash: Got it.

(Nash turns the music off.)

Lon: Thank you.

Nash: Hey, this is radio Lon. The LAST thing we want to be playing is the wrong music.

Lon: I don't want to be this person anymore.

Nash: Who do you want to be Lon? I mean you could be <u>me</u> but I live with my wife and kid and mother-in-law and there is definitely an odor problem. Who do you want to be?

Lon: That man in Tiananmen Square, you know the one, the small man standing in the road, alone, in front of this huge tank. He, he, he....stood there, somehow he stopped the tank with his arm. No. With his will. People had been killed in Tiananmen square, yet he, he stood firm. He had to stand in the tank's path, he had no choice; his message was clear...

Nash: What was that?

Lon: Stop.

Nash: On the call-in last week, you said you were finally <u>coming out</u>. Is that what I think it means?

Lon: Outside.

Nash: Ah outside. Good, 'cause Evansville is not THE PLACE to choose to "come out."

Lon: Outside.

Nash: And why come outside <u>now</u> Lon?

Lon: I'm tired.

Nash: Tired?

Lon: Tired of being a coward.

Nash: And what to do, now that you're outside? How do you overcome being the coward?

Lon: Stand in front of the tank.

Nash: Tiananmen Square?

Lon: Right.

Nash: And my show. Here. Tonight, is this YOUR Tiananmen Square?

Lon: I hope so.

Nash: And when, just when were you last outside?

Lon: I don't want to say.

Nash: You're my guest Lon. It's twenty minutes til midnight and this is my show and I say you can say.

Mooning Lon Chaney

Lon: I'm not proud of it.

Nash: Not proud of what?

Lon: How I've lived.

Nash: Who-tha-hell is? When were you last outside Lon?

Lon: Sixth grade.

Nash: Sixth grade?

Lon: Uh huh.

Nash: SIXTH GRADE?

Lon: I'm not proud of it.

Nash: I know, I know, I know; but how old are you now?

Lon: Twenties.

Nash: Okay, twenty-something.

Lon: I cleaned up a bit for tonight.

Nash: Didya?

Lon: I know, I know I haven't taken care of myself.

Nash: When did all this begin for you? What happened before the sixth grade?

Lon: Well I was doing <u>fine</u> up til the Third grade.

Nash: What happened in the third grade?

Lon: My neighbor, Miss Medley, was the sixth grade teacher. She owned a cat. a big orange male...<u>Tang</u>. Tang was top-cat in the neighborhood. Tang was fearless. Dogs were afraid of Tang. Tang was bigger than me, in a one-on-one wrestling match, Tang would pin me to the mat. No contest.

So it was quite a surprise when, one morning I was playing in the yard. Small town, everybody has a yard; anyway, suddenly this intelligent sixth-grade school teacher came screaming out of her front door, rushed to her yard, knelt down. Tang, lay dead. Mortally wounded, a big gash in his neck. Ripped open with authority. Miss Medley was distraught. I stared from a short distance. then, she got real quiet. She must've been wondering, "What happened? Who or what would have the guts to take on Tang?" Then with a quick cut of her head, she looked to me and pointed....<u>youuuu</u>.

Nash: Not, not really looking forward to the sixth grade were ya Lon?

Lon: I ran inside and hid under the wicker lounge chair.

Nash: So the world wants to know Lon, did you kill Tang?

Lon: I don't remember killing Tang.

Nash: But Miss Medley said you did.

Lon: I couldn't have.

Nash: But she pointed the finger at you.

Lon: I know.

Nash: A person of authority points the finger at a young kid, that kid begins to doubt. Doesn't he?

Lon: Yes.

Nash: This Medley-Teacher-Chick sounds dangerous.

Lon: Oh she was, she is. And well read. Well read teachers....do that.

Nash: I know, I live with one.

Lon: And superstitious and vindictive.

Nash: Sounds familiar.

Lon: One afternoon, shortly after Tang's death, I was out back, playing. Miss Medley was across the fence, her backyard. I didn't see her. She waited behind a bush til I got near. She grabbed my shirt, pulled me to the fence and decided it was her duty to educate me..."on June 11, 1590, a man was brought to trial having been accused of being a <u>Werewolf</u>. This filthy beast had murdered thirteen young children and ate their hearts panting, hot and raw, which he accounted dainty morsels and best agreeing to his appetite. His devilish and damnable deeds began as a child with the killing of <u>a neighbor's cat</u>."

Nash: She's got a strong case Lon.

Lon: I ran back inside under my wicker lounge chair. No way, there was <u>no</u> <u>way</u> I could ever enter the Sixth Grade.

Nash: So let's have it Lon...The truth about Tang.

Lon: I liked Tang. I did. I don't remember anything about that night he died. But that's my problem.

Nash: What's your problem?

Lon: Not remembering...Oh it's so clear, <u>so clear</u>.

Nash: Help us out.

Lon: My problem is, I remembered nothing about the night Tang died.

Nash: Right.

Lon: It just so happened, the day after a kill...."The Wolf Man" remembered nothing about the night before.

Nash: Lon, you just described my post-college-disco years.

Lon: My mother tried to protect me.

Nash: Yeah, what'd she do?

Lon: Took me outa school. Tied me to the wicker lounge chair.

Nash: Whoa! Watch out for MOM.

Lon: It was about this time that Fletcher Thornton and several cronies got in the habit of asking Fletcher's older brother Cleveland...Cleveland had a car...asking Cleveland to drive slowly past my house on full moon nights, for hours, allowing Fletcher and his cronies to roll down the windows, drop their jeans and moon...well, my mother liked to sit on the porch in the evening.

Nash: Oooh.

Lon: A devout Baptist.

Nash: Cleveland is going straight to hell.

Lon: The beer bottles crashing across the front porch; the howling, the mooning; I was burrowed deep under the wicker lounge chair; trying to block out my mother's screams, block out her condemnation; her incessant praying and what she called, her "coming apart." She did ya know. She came apart. My fault, my fault, my fault...

Nash: So after the sixth grade Lon; I'm afraid to ask...high school?

Lon: Under the wicker.

Nash: Evansville, if you've just joined us, you're listening to Nash-of-the-Nocturne Shift, WADO AM 660, fifteen minutes til midnight, with Lon Chaney tha third, battling his demon since childhood. He's come out to face the tank; to face Fletcher Thornton, wherever he is...

Lon: He went off to college. But his little brother...

Nash: They always have a little brother don't they.

Lon: Scott. With Scott, It got worse.

Nash: How'd it get worse?

Lon: Scott's class was the <u>largest</u> in school history.

Nash: Lemme guess, they all had cars.

Lon: Uh huh.

Nash: How did you deal with it Lon?

Lon: I went deeper. The wicker lounge chair was too shallow...I moved deeper, under the wicker sofa. But mother, dear mother was too big to hide under the wicker. She died. Drank herself to death. After that, I began digging through her things. Her trunks, her desk, her letters, old pictures, she had always kept from me. I read up on my family. My father. My grandfather. She had never talked about them. I thought if I could learn about them, I might understand what was happening to me.

Nash: And what did you learn Lon?

Lon: My grandfather...

Nash: Tha nut.

Lon: He could transform himself into anything. A popular nineteen twenties Hollywood joke was, "don't step on it, it might be Lon Chaney."

Nash: And your father, Junior?

Mooning Lon Chaney

Lon: Different.

Nash: What made him different?

Lon: Well, he was still-born.

Nash: That's different.

Lon: So my grandfather smashed the ice on Belle Isle Lake, plunging my father into the bitterly cold water to shock the life into him. By age three, my father was performing with him in an acrobatic act. Not long after that, his mother died and he was placed in a foster home. When my grandfather dropped him off at the foster home, he said, "Junior, you go inside now or you can go out back there to that wood shed, get me a board, and I'm going to hit you."

Nash: Lemme guess...

Lon: Junior went inside.

Nash: Lon, we're coming up on ten minutes til midnight.

Lon: Ten minutes?

Nash: That's right. Ten minutes til Midnight. Full moon shining down on Evansville. Are you gonna be alright? Are we all safe here?

Lon: I don't know, I don't know, I, I, I don't...?

Nash: Wrong answer Lon. What happened after the foster home?

95

Lon: Junior worked as a newsboy, apricot picker, a cattle slaughterer, a poultry dresser, and a boilermaker.

Nash: And your grandfather? The ole' ice-smasher-baby-plunger? What happened to him?

Lon: Oh he prospered.

Nash: Don't they always.

Lon: He was a major MGM star.

Nash: The original "Phantom of the Opera" wasn't he?

Lon: Yes... *(Lon quotes)* Los Angeles, Ca., Lon Chaney, the original, died of throat cancer the twelfth of July, 1930. *(to Nash)* Remember that date.

Nash: The twelfth of July?

Lon: That's today.

Nash: You're spooking me Lon.

Lon: What time is it?

Nash: Never mind; what happened to your father Lon?

Lon: You said ten minutes til midnight?

Nash: Forget about that. What happened to your dad Lon? what happened to Junior?

Lon: His father's death had set him free. After thirty-three years of heartbreak, He was free to achieve the part he would forever, proudly call "My Baby."

Nash: THE WOLF MAN.

Lon: Right. And he became the only monster to be played by the same actor; the only monster to find a cure; and the only monster to pass it on...

Nash: To you?

Lon: A lot of people think so.

Nash: Teachers, mooners and small town-cruisers. We know those people don't we Lon.

Lon: What if they're right?

Nash: Eight minutes til midnight my nocturnal listeners...Full moon shining down on Evansville. What's going to happen Lon?

Lon: This is big for me.

Nash: Big for you? Lemme tell ya about big, I'm sitting here with the ghost of Tang whispering over my shoulder, things that happened to him at midnight; things I don't want to hear. So I'll ask again Lon...am I safe?

Lon: Was the man in Tiananmen Square safe?

Nash: Me? Us? Here? Now? Are we safe?

Lon: *(quotes)* San Clemente, California, 1973: Lon Chaney Jr. died of a heart attack. It was the twelfth of July. *(To Nash)* A week later, I was born.

Nash: Bad timing Lon.

Lon: I know. But the worst was yet to come.

Nash: What could be worse?

Lon: <u>Sixth grade</u>.

Nash: Oh shit. Miss Medley.

Lon: Uh huh.

Nash: Bugaboo Bitch from Hell.

Lon: Yep.

Nash: What'd she do to you?

Lon: She liked to seat her pupils in alphabetical order, which looked good for me, 'cause "Chaney" wouldn't be up front; actually, "Wolf Man" would've placed me in the very back of the room, Better, I thought but she decided, in memory of Tang, to assign me a place she could keep an eye....Front row.

My existence there can only be described in two words: sweating bullets. *(a beat)* Silver bullets.

Nash: That's uh...

Lon: Uh huh.

Mooning Lon Chaney

Nash: That's a joke isn't it Lon?

Lon: I can be funny.

Nash: My job. My job Lon.

Lon: I'm sorry.

Nash: For those listening who may be unaware: You could only
kill the Werewolf with a silver bullet. Sweating silver bullets
here Evansville. Nash of the Nocturne Shift, three minutes
til midnight. WADO AM 660 pushing, pulling, playing the
wrong music, doing whatever it takes to help Tiananmen
Lon here come out and face the tank.

Not much time Lon.

Lon: 'Never is.

Nash: Talk to me.

Lon: It was always a puzzle.

Nash: A puzzle?

Lon: The dates. The dates, the killer dates.

Nash: Eat something else. What dates?

Lon: Beginning in 1590, the werewolf's obituary read: "A most
wicked Sorcerer was taken and executed the twelfth of July!

Nash: That's...that's the....

Lon: Date they all died.

Nash: The twelfth of July.

Lon: Today.

Nash: Right.

Lon: And you booked me here today.

Nash: Whoa. Correction: Our Producer booked you.

Lon: You booked me.

Nash: *(yells offstage)* Stephanie?

Lon: What time is it?

Nash: Somebody get her out here!

Lon: What time...? What time is it? What time is it...?

Nash: One minute til Midnight.

> *Lon checks his hands and neck.*

Lon: You're beaten, beaten to the punch.

Nash: Easy now... *(yells offstage)* Steph...?

Lon: Your nerves have been beaten to the punch.

Nash: Stay with me Lon.

Lon: You don't have time; you think you do; you think you do, but you don't.

Nash: Twenty seconds.

Mooning Lon Chaney

Lon: First thing that goes? Nervous system. Zip.

Nash: Look at me Lon.

Lon: Zip. gone.

Nash: Repeat after me: I AM SPARTACUS!

Lon: Zip. gone.

Nash: Okay, try this: I AM TIANANMEN LON and I'm mad
    as hell...

Lon: How do I look?

Nash: And I'm not gonna take it anymore.

Lon: How do I look? Tell Me How I Look?

Nash: You look...

Lon: I don't feel so good.

Nash: You look fine.

Lon: What time is it? What time is it? WHAT TIME IS IT?

Nash: It's...it's midnight.

Lon: I'm changing, I'm changing, I'm changing...

Nash: Lon...?

Lon: It's happening.

Nash: Nothing's happening.

Lon: Look, Look at my neck.

Nash: This is your moment Lon.

Lon: I'm changing.

Nash: Your moment. Don't let it pass.

Lon: I'm changing...

Nash: Speak now...

   (Lon is frozen in fear.)

Nash: Speak now Lon. It's Tiananmen Square. You're standing
   in front of the tank.

Lon: They're not stopping.

Nash: Say it.

Lon: They're not stopping, the cars are not stopping...

Nash: Look at me, look at me Lon.

Lon: It's too late.

Nash: It's not too late.

Lon: It's too late.

Nash: Tiananmen Square! Remember The Man? You wanted to
   be like him. What did he do? What did he say Lon? Say it.
   <u>Say-it</u>.

   (Lon is frozen in fear. Nash patiently waits…then puts

his hand over the microphone.)

Nash: *(to someone offstage)* That's it. We lost 'im.

> *(Nash takes off his headphones. Looks away from Lon and shrugs to his producer. Lon, sweaty and frightened, leans to the microphone, speaks softly but with deep resolve.)*

Lon: Stop.

Nash: Whatwasthat?

Lon: Stop.

Nash: Say-it-again.

Lon: Stop.

Nash: Ddn't hear ya.

Lon: Stop.

Nash: Give me more.

Lon: Stop.

Nash: More.

Lon: STOP. STOP. STOOOOOOP.

> *(Lon sits back. Exhausted.)*

Nash: And they will.

> *(Lights fade to Gypsy violin music. Soft Bkgd.)*

ty adams

(A soft spotlight remains on Lon.)

(Nash speaks from darkness.)

Nash: That's it my nocturnal creatures; you've been listening to Nash of the Nocturne Shift, WADO AM 660 on your dial; broadcasting from the skirts of Evans... no, make that LIVE from Tiananmen Square....I bid <u>you</u> peace.

(Blackout. Music up.)

end of play

Touch

ty adams

Touch was first presented at The 42nd Street Theatre, New York City, in October, 2000 with the following cast:

Sonya	Linda Larsen
Murphy	Joe Mortimer
Isabel	Courtney Rohler
Hector	Steven Ogg
Yoshi	Kiki Moritsugu

Directed by Kelly Kimball
Stage Manager Gemeem Davis

Touch

characters

Sonya...............flawed.

A witchy, glamorous woman; black dress against alabaster skin, disheveled hair and love-me-love-my-glasses.

Murphy............searching.

The-successful-guy-next-door? No. His I-got-nuthin' little brother.

Isabel...............perfect.

A mass of modern energy in skin-hugging white leggings, tan and healthy.

Hector............lost.

A wannabe hot-blooded, shirtless Latino hunk roasting marshmallows over a smoldering mattress. NOT.

Yoshi............. ...tempest...with a tea pot. A young oriental tea master trainee in japanese kimono, split white socks with a soft voice, an easy smile and about to explode.

scene: New York City and The Catskill Mountains

• Isabel's bedroom; a trendy street; upper west side Manhattan

• Mi Cocina Restaurant; lower Manhattan

- A log cabin in the Catskill Mountains

- A tatami tea room in the Catskills

- A funeral parlor in one of the boroughs - New York City

time: any minute

the set : one piece / nothing moves

> - Bedroom: a bed stage right, horizontal to the audience; upstage center, a closet door (used as an entrance for all dream or fantasy scenes)
>
> - Log Cabin: Same bed stripped of its covers.
>
> - Restaurant: two stools stage left.
>
> - Tea Room: bare stage space between bedroom and restaurant.
>
> - Funeral: Bare stage space between bedroom and restaurant.

Touch

SCENE.... (Isabel's bedroom. a spotlight appears on the face of Isabel; she is lounging across the bed, facing the audience; her face covered with a green yogurt and avocado facial mask.

Murphy, in the background, is packing; back and forth to the closet, to the suitcase on the bed's edge. He carelessly stuffs items taken from the closet. Isabel is cool and calm.)

Isabel: *(to us)* Look at 'im...

> *(Lights up full to reveal Murphy)*

Isabel: *(to us)* Oh, you don't know this...he <u>never</u> <u>packs</u> because he <u>never</u> <u>leaves</u>... look at him; he's never moved this fast in his life; you'd think he couldn't wait to get out of here; do I exaggerate? Of course. That's the way I am; is anything wrong with that? Of course not; that's the way it is; the way I am is the way it is and if that's not good enough well he can just...oh he hasn't said he's leaving, no, but...

> *(a glance his way; Murphy continues packing)*

LITTLE THINGS give him away. *(to us)* A woman notices little things; she notices, she knows; that's how it works.

Murphy?

> *(Isabel claims a piece of clothing.)*

Mine.

> *(Murphy Hands the clothing to Isabel; continues packing;*

ty adams

Isabel does an air ballet with her legs, turns over on her back, looks away from Murphy but extends an arm to him.)

Mine.

(Murphy, irritated, looks to us; reluctantly hands her a white cap; Isabel flips over on her stomach and faces the audience; extends an arm to Murphy.)

Mine.

Murphy: You gave me this belt Isabel.

Isabel: <u>Loaned</u> the belt.

Murphy: It was a...

Isabel: Keyword: LOANED.

(Murphy gives her the belt.)

Isabel: Thank you.

(Murphy returns to packing; stops with a CD in his hand.)

Isabel: Anyway, as I was saying...

Murphy: MINE. How do I know it's mine Isabel? HOW DO I KNOW IT'S MINE? It's jazz. It's Sonny Rollins. SONNY ROLLINS. JAZZ. CD. MINE.

Isabel: Are you leaving me Murphy?   Is it Sonya?

Touch

(Murphy continues packing.)

Isabel: It is isn't it?

Murphy: It's not about Sonya.

Isabel: You were shaking.

Murphy: I WAS shaking.

Isabel: Because of HER.

Murphy: *(to us)* I shake at funerals, I'm sorry.

Isabel: You were WET with excitement.

Murphy: It was raining Isabel.

Isabel: There-is-wet-and-there-is-wet.

Murphy: (to us) It was raining.

Isabel: Do you love her?

Murphy: I don't know.

Isabel: YOU DON'T KNOW?

Murphy: Is there an echo?

Isabel: PICKING UP THE WIDOW AT THE FUNERAL?

Murphy: I didn't...

Isabel: Murphy...Bad taste.

Murphy: They were not married and you know it.

Isabel: *(to us)* We arrived at Hector's funeral late.

Murphy: *(to us)* I went in first.

Isabel: *(to us)* I went in first; after all, they met through me.

Murphy: *(to us)* Isabel had once introduced me to Hector, her lover at the time. That's why it seemed odd when she mentioned his funeral.

Isabel: Murphy...?

Murphy: Yes?

Isabel: A friend of mine is having a funeral.

Murphy: *(to us)* Sounds like a party.

Isabel: Wanna go?

Murphy: Sure, why not.

   (to us) He's dead. I'm next. I saw the movie.

Isabel: *(to the air)* Remember that movie with Betty Davis and the letter?

Murphy: She killed her lover.

Isabel: Uh huh.

Murphy: *(to us)* Checkmate!

Isabel: I love her movies.

Touch

Murphy: (to us) When I think of Isabel I think of a childlike, seemingly Victorian sense of innocence and something considerably darker; something so perfect that after awhile her surface stops breathing.

Isabel: Honey...?

Murphy: Yes...?

Isabel: Something's wrong with my surface.

Murphy: It's nothing sweetheart.

Isabel: It's something.

Murphy: You've just stopped breathing that's all.

Isabel: *(to us)* When I think of Murphy I think of rivulets of theatre paint, caked-on theatre paint; embossed, cake-icing frozen in the unhappy position; in essence: built-up globules.

Murphy: (to us) She's decorative...

Isabel: (to us) He's miserable...

Murphy: Isabel...?

Isabel: Yes...?

Murphy: Are you happy?

Isabel: All the time.

Murphy: *(to us)* THAT bothers me.

Isabel: I don't see anything wrong with being happy.

Murphy: All the time?

Isabel: Well...

Murphy: It's not natural Isabel.

Isabel: Happiness is NOT SPRING WATER Murphy.

Murphy: I'm glad you said that...

   (to us) fourteen bottles in the frig.

Isabel: I need that water.

Murphy: Spring water is ALL WE HAVE Isabel.

Isabel: Oh really? *(to us)* The frig is full of ORANGES.

Murphy: And don't attack my oranges.

Isabel: Tons of oranges.

Murphy: So?

Isabel: So you have a navel fetish Murphy.

Murphy: Navel fetish?

   (to us) She likes to push that "fetish" business; makes her feel normal.

Isabel: You should mention that to your therapist.

Murphy: *(to us)* She likes to push that too.

Touch

Isabel: You two can share a Citrus experience.

Murphy: Cute.

> *(to us)* Oranges aren't perfect, I like that; when there's a freeze in Florida and nobody wants the oranges with the navels outa place, I take them.

> Did you hear about that freeze in Florida Isabel?

Isabel: No; not really.

Murphy: Yep.

Isabel: I'll make room in the frig.

Murphy: Thank you.

Isabel: I feel uneasy about this Murphy.

Murphy: About what?

Isabel: There's a lot of color in the frig.

Murphy: *(to us)* She has this thing about <u>color</u>.

Isabel: A lot of orange.

Murphy: *(to us)* I'm sick of her obsession with white; perfectly white; this, this <u>puritanical-shit-paper's-gotta-be-white.</u>

Isabel: Murphy...?

Murphy: Yes?

Isabel: What's this <u>blue stuff</u> in the bathroom?

Murphy: Toilet paper sweetheart.

Isabel: I told you to get <u>white.</u>

Murphy: They-were-out-of-white-dear.

Isabel: Are you trying to be firm with me Murphy?

Murphy: No, I'm just trying to buy toilet paper.

Isabel: You know I need white. I need white, you get blue; my needs aren't being filled.

Murphy: *(to us)* Just once, JUST ONCE I'd like to see her in-need of a subway card.

Isabel: *(to the air)* TAXI.

Murphy: *(to us)* Recently I've resorted to desperate things...

    (a cautious look left and right.)

    (to us) Just to insert a flaw into our life I told her my parents were killed in a train crash.

Isabel: Oh dear.

Murphy: Coming home from skiing.

Isabel: Stratton?

Murphy: Sugarloaf.

Isabel: I go to Stratton.

Murphy: I broke my leg there once.

Isabel: Stratton?

Murphy: Sugarloaf.

    (to us) HELP ME.

Isabel: Which leg?

Murphy: Isabel....

Isabel: I know. You're afraid of happiness.

Murphy: Let me explain....

Isabel: Psychological hangup.

Murphy: Of course it's psychological.

Isabel: You're bringing excess baggage into this relationship.

Murphy: I suppose you think...

Isabel: Blame-it-on-the-parents...

Murphy: I'm not blaming...

Isabel: Can't do that.

Murphy: *(to us)* My parents are sick people. Their favorite phrase
    was "Stop it, you're having too much fun."

Isabel: My parents are so sweet.

Murphy: *(to us)* POUNDED INTO ME...

Isabel: They did this bus tour to Disney World...

Murphy: *(to us)* Can you have too much fun?

Isabel: My father's favorite phrase is..."What we have here is a RELATIONSHIP."

Murphy: Exactly. Relationships are improvised; imperfect; Where is it Isabel? WHERE IS IMPERFECT?

(Isabel looks at Murphy)

Isabel: *(to us)* Should I tell 'im?

Murphy: I have questions, doubts, Isabel.

Isabel: That's okay.

Murphy: No, it's not okay.

Isabel: You just need your bio-feedback inducts cleaned out.

Murphy: My what?

Isabel: Your BIO-FEEDBACK INDUCTS. I'll take you to Soho to my Japanese Tea Master.

Murphy: No.

Isabel: Afterwards you'll read "Dianetics" by L. Ron Hubbard.

Murphy: *(to us)* I'm-not-reading...

Isabel: I read it three times.

Murphy: Good for you.

Isabel: Okay you only have to read it once.

Murphy: Thank you.

Isabel: I'm so good to you.

Murphy: (to us) I'm gonna kill her; it's gonna be ugly.

Isabel: Murphy, remember the day we met?

Murphy: It's very vague right now sweetheart.

Isabel: Macy's....

Murphy: *(to us)* Probably the largest department store in the world.

Isabel: You were standing in Electronics on the fifth floor watching Jeopardy on the t.v. sets.

Murphy: *(to us)* It's free.

Isabel: I BREATHED on your neck...

   (Murphy smiles)

Isabel: You smiled.

Murphy: I smiled because I knew the Jeopardy question Isabel.

Isabel: The contestants were lost, remember?

Murphy: *(to the air)* What was it....? Uhhh, oh yes, "This ancient civilization believed that before men and women existed, humans were one."

BOTH: *(face to face)* WHO WERE THE GREEKS?

Isabel: (to the air) I love mythology. We could've had a marriage made in heaven sharing moments like that.

Murphy: *(to us)* That was the ONLY MOMENT.

I'm leaving you Isabel.

Isabel: Get to the point Murphy.

Murphy: I'm-leaving-you-Isabel.

Isabel: Why would you do that?

Murphy: You're out of touch.

Isabel: I'm not out of touch.

(to us) I'm not; watch this....

Murphy...?

Murphy: Yes dear?

Isabel: I'm worried about the Knicks.

Murphy: You ARE...?

Isabel: They had a terrible season last year.

Murphy: I know...

Isabel: I thought one draft pick was smart.

Murphy: It was; on paper it looked good but...

Isabel: We need a big guy in the center...

Touch

Murphy: God I know. Stupid, just stupid.

Isabel: And what's with the coaching changes?

Murphy: Insane.

Isabel: Everybody knows...

Murphy: We all know.

Isabel: What we really need is A COACH.

Murphy: Phil Jackson.

Isabel: I was thinkin' Phil.

Murphy: A former Knick.

Isabel: Makes sense.

Murphy: Bingo!   Bring-Him-Home.

Isabel: Won't happen.

   (to us) then I fucked up...

   Honey...?

Murphy: Yes?

Isabel: I've always wondered....what IS-a-Knick?

Murphy: *(to us)* Hey, It's like jazz...."if you have to ask..."

   A Knick is a basketball player Isabel.

Isabel: Ohhh...

(to us) Asshole. I knew that.

Murphy: I wouldn't worry about it Isabel; think about something important.

Isabel: *(to the air)* What to wear to the funeral?

(to us) My black isn't FUNERAL BLACK if you know what I mean.

Murphy: *(to us)* We arrived late for Hector's funeral...

(Lights change; they move to the bare space center stage; Sonya appears from stage left; stands in front of stools dressed in black, veiled and mysterious. Murphy and Isabel converse throughout funeral, at times inappropriately loud, then hushed realizing their situation.)

Isabel: (to us) I flew in; two weeks on a modeling shoot in Mexico; I do Makeup.

Murphy: *(to us)* I had been doing a revival of "Love Letters" at the Promenade with what's-her-name Uhhh...Elizabeth McGovern; actually Nathan Lane had a cold and they weren't sure if he'd go on; well, I mean in this biz your body is your instrument and a cold can be serious.

(Murphy breaks down, cries)

Isabel: Murphy? Are you okay?

Murphy: Nathan Lane went on.

Isabel: I thought you said...

Murphy: I never did "Love Letters."

Isabel: You what?

Murphy: The SON OF A BITCH went on, contaminating everybody; I HATE HIS GUTS.

Isabel: Shhhh....

Murphy: I hadn't worked for months. I HATE HIS FUCKIN' GUTS; he's not right for the part anyway; okay, okay, okay, I know everybody does "Love Letters" BUT NOT WITH A COLD.

Isabel: Murphy take it easy.

Murphy: I get so upset just thinking about it.

Isabel: It's okay, it's okay.

Sonya: Shhhh....

Murphy: *(in Sonya's direction)* I'm sorry.....

Isabel: *(in Sonya's direction)* He's sorry...he misses Hector <u>so much</u>.

Murphy: This is embarrassing....

Isabel: Murphy....? Where were you those WEEKS you were supposed to be doing "Love Letters"?

(Murphy, a guilty look to us. **Blackout funeral**. *They quickly return to the bedroom, Murphy continues packing.)*

Isabel: Where were you Murphy? With Sonya? Were you with Sonya? When I think of sweating my buns off in Mexico...

Murphy: Ha. PUERTO VALLARTA.

Isabel: Eating terrible food; wrapping models in sea algae; wallowing in beach sand FOR WHAT?

Murphy: *(to us)* One word...MONEY.

Isabel: That does it.

(Isabel slams the suitcase)

Isabel: GET OUT MURPHY.

Murphy: What happened to us Isabel?

Isabel: It begins with an S.

Murphy: We, we could never, never connect. We wanted to, WE WANTED TO BUT...

Isabel: Stop it Murphy....

Murphy: Look at us now...

Isabel: Yeah, picking up women at funerals.

Murphy: *(to us)* Ah! Sonya was wearing this black...

Touch

Isabel: *(to us)* Oh cheap black dress.

Murphy: *(to us)* And her skin, her skin was, was, was...

Isabel: And what was wrong with this woman's skin?

Murphy: *(to us)* Her skin was trembling alabaster...

Isabel: *(to us)* She had an Avenue-D-tar-beach-tan and it wasn't trembling..

.Murphy: *(to us)* She was from another world; Isabel felt it too.

Isabel: Murphy?

Murphy: Yes?

Isabel: Sonya isn't from around here is she?

Murphy: No, Texas I think.

Isabel: I heard Hector picked her up at the ZOO of all places.

Murphy: *(to us)* Botanical gardens....

Isabel: A waitress...

Murphy: *(to us)* Actress.

Isabel: Has-been-from-small-town Texas.

Murphy: *(to us)* Traveled around a lot; father in the military.

Isabel: She could use a little shadow around those cheekbones.

Murphy: *(to us)* Was once Miss Soft Shell Crab of Galveston, Texas.

Isabel: Someone said she was allergic to yellow?

Murphy: *(to us)* Sensitive.

Isabel: She looks like she's been here forever.

Murphy: (to us) Fifteen years in New York; lots of acting classes...

BOTH: STUDIED WITH UTA HAGEN.

Murphy: (to us) When I think of Sonya I think, I think of those oranges in Florida after a freeze; flawed but an-almost-cartoon-softness, smoothness, as if she had licked her flaws into a polished armor and then crafted that armor into another skin.

Isabel: She survived. Hector died. I hate her.

Murphy: Not her fault. Did you read in the paper about the crash?

Isabel: No.

   (to us) He knows I hate newsprint; it rubs off on my hands.

   (Murphy produces a newspaper clipping..reads.)

Murphy: Her companion, a Mr. Hector Prado, film director representing Rosario Cinematografica out of Mexico City....was driving.

Isabel: I don't care. The bitch walked away with a few bruises.

Murphy: *(to us)* So after the funeral...

Isabel: *(to us)* I flew back to Mexico.

Murphy: *(to us)* I sat around...

       (tele rings)

Isabel: *(on phone)* Hi honey, any calls?

Murphy: (on phone) No.

   (to us) I lied.

      (tele rings)

      (Sonya appears on a stool at Mi Cocina Restaurant. Lighting is reduced to two spots, Murphy and Sonya; they direct their phone conversation to us.)

Sonya: Murphy?

Murphy: Yes...?

Sonya: It's Sonya.

Murphy: Sonya?

Sonya: You may not remember me...

Murphy: Yes. You and I auditioned for uhhh...

Sonya: Hector.

Murphy: Right.

Sonya: I saw you the other day at his funeral; you were very distraught.

Murphy: Oh that, that was.....how, how are you?

Sonya: I'm falling apart.

Murphy: Talk-to-me.

Sonya: I can't....

Murphy: Give me something.

Sonya: I, I can't; it's toooo...

Murphy: Anything...

Sonya: I'm, I'm allergic to yellow...

Murphy: I think that's wonderful.

Sonya: It began with yellow dye in makeup then grew into something bigger.

Murphy: It feels SO GOOD to meet someone else who has allergies.

Sonya: That's only the beginning.

Murphy: Spare me nothing.

Sonya: We're doin' a hundred miles an hour in the Lincoln Tunnel...Hector's driving.

Touch

Murphy: Omigod.

> *(Hector enters. Takes the other stool beside Sonya; his eyes ahead and his hands on the wheel.)*

Sonya: We were drinkin' a lot. He gets angry when he drinks; he gets angry when he drives; he's an angry man, anyway, sometimes you just stare at 'im.

Hector: What are you staring at Sonya?

Sonya: *(to us)* Easy.

I'm staring at you dear.

Hector: You're a hopeless romantic aren't you Sonya?

Sonya: *(to us)* I am.

Hector: I'll bet you like Earth colors...

Sonya: *(to us)* I do.

Hector: Foggy nights and rainy days...

Sonya: *(to us)* What-can-I-say...

Hector: Lina Wertmuller films and pink candles burning when you make love.

Sonya: *(to us)* Doesn't everybody...

Hector: I can't give you those things Sonya.

Sonya: *(to us)* So what else is new?

That's okay Hector honey...

Hector: I'm too worried about the economy...

Sonya: *(to us)* Poor guy; he means ecology.

Hector: People are fuckin' up the ozone layer with chemical plants and feminine hygiene spray.

Sonya: Hector, it's a woman's right to use...

Hector: Feminine hygiene spray is fuckin' up the ozone.

Sonya: Slow down Hector...

Hector: I'm pissed off okay.

Isabel: Be pissed off but slow.

Hector: I AM PISSED-OFF OKAY?

Isabel: (to us) That didn't work...

Did you remember to pay those speeding tickets Hector?

Hector: Fuck 'em. I'm going to court.

Sonya: Going to court for speeding tickets?

Hector: I'm going to plead temporary insanity.

Sonya: (to us) Why bother with "temporary".

That sounds like good legal strategy honey.

(to Murphy) that's when he unscrewed the knob on the stick shift which was not the unscrewing type and began waving this eightball in my face which was annoying because of the hundred-miles-per-hour-thing and then I saw it.....the eightball was...

Murphy: Yellow?

Sonya: Yep.

Murphy: Bastard.

Sonya: Eightballs are supposed to be black aren't they?

Murphy: Some fall into the wrong hands.

Sonya: Suddenly we come out of the tunnel; a truck had stalled; Hector was looking at me; I was looking at the truck; I looked at Hector; he's still looking at me; "Watch the road Hector honey." WATCH THE ROAD... "

(Sound of Car crash. Blackout Stools; lights up bedroom.)

Murphy: *(to us)* After that call from Sonya, I don't know, I became, became uhhh....

(phone rings; Isabel appears; they speak to the air)

Isabel: Murphy....?

Murphy: Yes...?

Isabel: You've been rather quiet lately when I call.

Murphy: You exaggerate.

Isabel: I don't think so.

Murphy: How's Mexico?

Isabel: Hot. Send my favorite water.

Murphy: *(to us)* Isn't Mexico surrounded by three oceans of water?

Murphy: Anything else dear?

Isabel: *(to us)* He always does this to me...

Why? Am I overlooking something?

Murphy: No, just asked.

Isabel: I can't think of anything else.

Murphy: I'll send the water.

Isabel: Thanks.

BOTH: Byyyyee...

Murphy: (to us) The next day...I was walking around pissed off because I didn't get the "Love Letters" job; I decided to get something to eat; there she was...

(Sonya appears sitting on a stool nursing a cup of tea.)

Murphy: Looking out the window at Mi Cocina Restaurant; a hopeless romantic on a rainy day.... THIS WOMAN was thinking <u>deep</u> thoughts.

Touch

Sonya: *(to herself)* <u>What</u> <u>to</u> <u>eat</u>?

> *(Murphy walks toward her.)*

Murphy: Hello again...

Sonya: 'Cuse me?

Murphy: Remember me?

Sonya: I know you, you're...

Murphy: Murphy.

Sonya: Right.

Murphy: You called me after the funeral...

Sonya: Purging thyself call.

Murphy: "Lena Wertmuller films and pink candles"...

Sonya: Oh my god, I said that?

Murphy: Uh huh.

Sonya: Sit down; I'm trying to figure things out.

> *(Murphy sits)*

Sonya: Since Hector's death I've been asking myself so many questions like, like, why didn't God tell Adam and Eve about heaven and hell? Why did God use a rib to create Eve? How many ribs did Adam have left? How many ribs did Caine have? How many ribs do I have? Do I owe someone a rib? If I order ribs in this restaurant, will something terrible happen? What the hell was bothering the serpent? Was he jealous? Was he nauseated? *(gasp)* Was the serpent even a <u>he</u>?

Murphy: (to us) This woman had A LOT of questions.

<u>Snake.</u>

Sonya: I-beg-ya-pardon...?

Murphy: The serpent was a <u>snake</u>.

Sonya: Interesting; then why did Charlton Heston get to play Moses? Was Marlon Brando too young?

Murphy: *(to us)* This woman is FAR FROM PERFECT.

Charlton Heston could grow a beard.

Sonya: *(into his eyes)* Really?

(to us) He was SOOO nice, I HAD to say....

(into his eyes).....really?

Murphy: Really. Listen, I'm sorry about Hector.

Sonya: I didn't know him, REALLY KNOW HIM; know what I mean?

Murphy: Did anybody?

Sonya: He said he knew Louie Malle, french director Louie Malle; he said Louie Malle once told him, "Hec, the world is getting noisier; noise creates energy and <u>this</u> <u>energy</u>..."

Murphy: "Is film."

Sonya: You knew Louie Malle?

Murphy: *(to us)* I lied...

    Yes.

Sonya: Hector never knew Louie Malle did he?

Murphy: No.

Sonya: Was he really from Mexico?

Murphy: *(to us)* Louie Malle is from France.

Sonya: Was he...?

Murphy: Pardon...?

Sonya: Was Hector from Mexico?

Murphy: Oh Hector, no, no, no...Poughkeepsie.

Sonya: Poughkeepsie?

Murphy: Uh huh.

Sonya: Well that explains it.

Murphy: What?

Sonya: His conversion to Transcendental Zoroastrianism.

Murphy: *(to us)* Now we're getting somewhere.

Sonya: Very seventies.

Murphy: I was into Post-Nam Buddhism in the seventies.

Sonya: (to us) SHALLOW

> Really? That sounds sooo deeep. Post-Nam Buddhism....wow.
>
> *(Murphy shrugs)*

Sonya: And now?

Murphy: Western Catskill Zen.

Sonya: OUUUH.

> (to us) He's getting better.

Murphy: And you?

Sonya: Southern Baptist.

Murphy: Southern...that's, that's, that's...

> (to us) No Fucking Way.

Sonya: Don't worry I've changed to the pre-Christian, nature-based Craft of the Goddess.

Murphy: *(to us)* Nature-based, very modern.

Touch

Sonya: It honors the nature and the power of women.

Murphy: *(to us)* What a magnificent creature!

Sonya: In The Craft of the Goddess the Seers vowed that A WOMAN would rise from the black ashes of death and become the new horizon, the new bridge to everlasting life; THAT WOMAN...

Murphy: *(to us)* Is sitting right next to me.

Sonya: I even thought of changing my name to Star Hawk.

Murphy: DO IT!

Sonya: (to us) Let's see how far he'll go...

I'm gonna let the hair under my arms grow to my knees; adrift in the summer; a single braid in the winter.

Murphy: DO IT!

Sonya: *(to us)* FINALLY, a shallow, follow-me-anywhere, western cat who sees a snake as a snake.

Murphy: *(to us)* FINALLY, a live, savagely real, flawed woman; I wanted sustained postprandial sex, either at her place or mine, or, if need be, in the form of mutual manual stimulation right here in the restaurant.

Sonya: All of this has made me very hungry.....are we alone?

Murphy: Yes.

(Sonya removes her sweater.)

137

Sonya: We begin with a duet of pastry packages in champagne sauce...

(Murphy unbuttons his shirt.)
Murphy: Crawfish Etoufée...

Sonya: Crab and cucumber filled with lobster and snow peas.

Murphy: New Orleans gumbo with orso and cabbage in a nut-brown roux.

(Sonya slips out of one shoe.)

Sonya: Fettuccine floating on top of braised Redfish Couvillion...

Murphy: I LOVE REDFISH COUVILLION!

(Sonya unzips her pants. Murphy removes a shoe.)

Sonya: Smoked duck breast with miso and green peppercorn sauce...

(Murphy tears his shirt off.)

Murphy: Steamed pork with star anise apple and quince...

Sonya: I'm still hungry.

(Murphy unzips his pants.)

Murphy: Now for the main course...

Sonya: Give Me The Main, Give Me The Main Murphy!

(Sonya slips out of another shoe.)

Touch

Murphy: The best bombolotti...

Sonya: I love bombolotti.

> *(Murphy removes his pants.)*

Murphy: Tossed in a sublime combination of crumbled sweet fennel sausage...

Sonya: Cognac and cream...

Murphy: A flash of hot sweeps across the palate...

Sonya: Priming you for more.

> *(Sonya easing out of her pants.)*

> *(Murphy throws his pants over his shoulder.)*

Murphy: Ease the cork out of a bottle of Chateau Mouton Rothschild...

Sonya: Nineteen-seventy-five...

Murphy: The Andy Warhol Label.

BOTH: He didn't even drink.

> *(Sonya tosses her pants.)*

> *(Sonya turns off the lamp. The cafe is dim.)*

Murphy: Oh yeah.

Sonya: Tell me Murphy, Have you ever been to Bali?

<header>

ty adams

</header>

Murphy: No but I can spiritually identify with Bali.

Sonya: Talk to me...

Murphy: The sky.

Sonya: The mountains...

Murphy: The smell...

Sonya: The view...

Murphy: The feel...

Sonya: The taste...

Murphy: BALI!

Sonya: I feel so neglected.

Murphy: It's so dark.

Sonya: Think of me as braille.

Murphy: You are braille.

Sonya: Weee...

Murphy: That-is-to-say, you and I...

Sonya: Feel the same things.

Murphy: That's it; we understand...

Sonya: Each other.

Murphy: As if we're...

Sonya: Joined together.

Murphy: That's it.

Sonya: Joined together, sharing, sharing, sharing...

Murphy: Bodies.

Sonya: Bodies?

Murphy: Bodies.

Sonya: Desires.

Murphy: I like bodies.

Sonya: Desires.

Murphy: Okay, okay, okay desires...

Sonya: Desires that we kept secret in, in, in...

Murphy: In the past.

Sonya: Denying ourselves...

Murphy: That's it; denying ourselves, denying ourselves the right to, to, to....

Sonya: To be together.

Murphy: I like that.

Sonya: To be together for, for, for....

Murphy: Forever.

Sonya: For the moment.

Murphy: Forever.

Sonya: For the moment.

Murphy: Okay, okay for the moment but, but with, with, with...

Sonya: With....

Murphy: WITH PASSION!

Sonya: A little passion.

Murphy: Passion and, and, and...

Sonya: Protection.

Murphy: Protection?

Sonya: Protection from, from, from...

Murphy: from the rain.

Sonya: *(to us)* From the rain?

Murphy: And, and the wind in our hair as, as we make love on the beach.

Sonya: *(to us)* Let's see how far he'll go?

Murphy: The sand grinding, grinding, grinding for, for, for....

Sonya: For as long as it takes a single bird to fly all the Earth's sand to the moon...

Touch

Murphy: Wow.

Sonya: One grain at a time.

Murphy: *(to us)* That's a long time.

Sonya: Let's get outa here Murphy.

Murphy: My place or yours?

Sonya: <u>Who</u> <u>tha-hell</u> <u>cares!</u>

> *(A sudden burst of music. preferably steamy saxophone jazz. They exit in a mad dash.)*

SCENE... (lights up bedroom; Isabel curls up in bed.)

Isabel: *(to us)* This is when it happens; when you're alone, in bed, late at night; your whole life just seems to... do I sound...? Omigod, do I sound unhappy? Do I exaggerate? Of course, that's what I do. I'm not unhappy, I'm sleepy.

> *(She falls asleep; Hector appears from the closet in a blue haze.)*

Hector: *(to us)* LISTEN TO ME. I swear on the breast of little Isa as she sleeps, I, Hector Prado, will clear my name of these lies. YES LIES.

For example: "Watch the road Hector honey." first of all Sonya would never say that to me; never; she would never call me honey; she would say something like, "Hec...", she liked to call me Hec; she would say, "Hec, what road is this?" She might say something like that.

143

And lemme-tell-you, lemme-tell-you...there is nothing wrong with a yellow eightball. NOTHING WRONG MAN. Lots of people have them around, you know? And another thing...ME? Little Hec? An ozone freak? I like feminine hygiene spray. Gimme a break man; I know what you're thinkin', I know, you're thinkin' Mexico City, air pollution and everything. LIES. Lemme-tell-you-lemme-tell-you...it all began when I flew to New York for a few days...

(Hector wakes her)

Hector: My little Isa?

Isabel: *(sits up in bed)* Hector, is that you?

Hector: Who-else?

Isabel: In town for a few days?

Hector: You-got-it my little chiquita.

Isabel: Then I suppose you're...

Hector: On to L.A.

Isabel: Right. Big movie deal?

Hector: BIG.

Isabel: *(to us)* <u>Liar</u>. He told me his movies were being shown at six-hundred drive-ins across Mexico on any given Saturday night; I was just in Mexico; there aren't six hundred drive-ins left in the world.

Touch

Hector: Isa...?

Isabel: Yes Hector?

Hector: Did you see my movies when you were in Mexico?

Isabel: No honey, I had to work.

Hector: *(to us)* Lies. She was at a coastal resort fucking some photographer on top of pseudo-Conran furniture; don't get me wrong, I LOVE CONRAN'S but in Mexico, the quality, you know.

Isabel: So what's the New York deal?

Hector: the deal is a joint venture with Crystal Falls Films; I'd direct the first film representing my company Rosario Cinematografica.

Isabel: And the script?

Hector: An <u>original</u> of mine.

Isabel: Hector, this script sounds familiar.

Hector: Isa, why don't you stick to makeup okay.

Isabel: It reminds me of that nineteen-fifty-eight cult classic...

Hector: *(to us)* Which was a piece of shit.

Isabel: JUNGLE JIM VERSUS KEMO THE TREE MONSTER.

Hector: So I made a few changes.

Isabel: You have butchered a cult classic!!

Hector: I gave it CLASS.

(to us) JORGE OF THE JUNGLE...a tight budget forced me to think about shooting the exteriors at the New York Botanical Gardens; that's where I first saw Sonya.

(Sonya appears in the doorway of the closet holding a newspaper; a spot on her; stage dims.)

Isabel: See anyone at the gardens today Hector?

Hector: No.

(to us) But what I saw was an <u>artist</u>, refining her craft; she was standing THIS CLOSE to an oriental plum tree...

Sonya: *(to us)* You're a tree. I don't care. Did you read this? Made the cover of the Post. Stay with me on this one...

Miss Taiwan had just won the Miss Asia Pageant; the other contestants said she was A FAKE; they attacked her, ripping her eyelashes from her face, only they weren't fake; She ran; they chased her, took her tiara and gave it to the runner-up; without eyelashes she didn't have a chance in Taiwan, it's a tough town; look at this poor woman; LASHLESS on the front page of the New York Post; her last words in bold type: "DEATH, IT IS SO QUICK."

(Closet door slams shut. Sonya is gone. lights up bedroom.)

146

Touch

Hector: (to us) Did you see the way she...ah. I had found my leading lady! Now, for the leading man I was thinking of Lorenzo Lamas but with a tight budget I was forced into a read-through with Nathan Lane...

Isabel: Uh 'cuse me, Nathan Lane has a cold.

Hector: Good; he's not right for the part anyway.

Isabel: Oh come on; Nathan is a wonderful actor.

Hector: Isa, lemme-tell-ya, lemme-tell-ya; in my adaptation, Jorge would be a stretch for Nathan Lane; he's a, he's a fine actor don't get me wrong but to reach JORGE, to reach that chili-pepper high....

Isabel: I know, you need A HOT BLOODED SHIRTLESS LATINO HUNK ROASTING MARSHMALLOWS OVER A SMOLDERING MATTRESS.

Hector: Lorenzo-Lamas!

Isabel: Honey, Crystal Falls called today; Nathan Lane has a cold so they're sending this other guy...

Hector: Lorenzo Lamas?

Isabel: Well, not exactly.

> *(Closet door opens; a spot on Murphy; lights dim on bedroom.)*

Hector: Okay, places, places everyone.

(Murphy and Sonya enter and stand center stage in the bare space; a tight spot encircles their faces cheek to cheek; Murphy is wearing a safari khaki shirt; Sonya in a doctor's white smock, a stethoscope around her neck; the scene should resemble the melodramas of the 1930's.)

Hector: (from darkness) JORGE OF THE JUNGLE. Scene I. Take I. The place: A medical outpost in the jungle somewhere outside the city limits of Rangoon, Burma. The time: LATE. Two lovers anticipate a romantic interlude while danger lurks beyond the shadows of camp; sounds of exotic birds fill the air; a full moon shines across the Amazon.

Murphy: Can we, can we stop for a sec...?

Hector: What is it?

Murphy: The Amazon doesn't flow through Rangoon, Burma.

Hector: So?

Murphy: It flows thru Brazil.

Hector: Thank you Mr. Murphy.

Murphy: I just thought...

Hector: Don't think Mr. Murphy.

Murphy: *(to Sonya)* It's just possibly the longest river in the world.

Hector: Jorge of the Jungle; TAKE TWO: A full moon shines across <u>The</u> <u>Amazon</u>. Little Rangoon-Burma-sweat-patches are forming under your arms; Jorge nudges his safari hat back on his head annnd ACTION...

Murphy: Kiss me Marion.

Sonya: No, I, I can't.

Murphy: Why not?

Sonya: I'm dedicated to my work.

Murphy: What's that got to do with kissing?

Sonya: I've dedicated my life to Rev. Cameron, to the Clinic, to the Jungle.

Murphy: 'Cuse me...

Hector: Yes Mr. Murphy?

Murphy: I should, I should take the hat off don'tchthink? It's hot, everybody's got sweat patches...

Hector: Mr. Murphy....

Murphy: Yes?

Hector: IMPROVISE.

Murphy: Improvise?

Sonya: Improvise.

Murphy: Okay...

Hector: TAKE THREE: Marion, a dedicated doctor from New York here on a mission, serenely closes her eyes anticipating romance. Sweet violins fill the air. Quiet Please.....annnnnnd ACTION!

Murphy: Kiss me Marion.

Sonya: No, I, I can't.

Murphy: Why not?

Sonya: I'm dedicated to my work.

Murphy: I have a question...

Hector: CUUUUT.

Murphy: Just, just one thing.

Hector: What is it?

Murphy: Why is Jorge asking...? I mean this guy wouldn't ask, he'd just kiss her.

Hector: Too contemporary for you Mr. Murphy?

Murphy: 'Cuse me? "Sweet violins fill the air" is contemporary?

Sonya: Hector....can we, can we take a break?

Hector: Take Five.

Sonya: Thank you.

Touch

(Sonya gyrates; loosens up; Murphy broods.)

Murphy: *(sarcastic)* Contemporary.....

Sonya: Murphy honey, we can do this.

Murphy: I know that but....

Sonya: You're too tense.

Murphy: I'M NOT too tense.

Sonya: Try breathing. Remember breathing?

Murphy: I remember breathing; I KNOW HOW TO BREATHE THANK YOU.

Sonya: *(pause, caressing)* breathe, from the not-so-fake eyelashes of Miss Taiwan down, down past those tense, ohhh very tense buns, soon-to-be-loose-buns; down to your toes; drain each blood vessel.... think spaghetti.

> *(Murphy rolls his neck, very loose now.)*

Hector: Okay, okay, okay...what's happenin'?

Sonya: are we...?

Murphy: Spaghetti.

Sonya: *(yells)* We're ready.

Hector: *(from darkness)* OKAY, PLACES EVERYONE; just pick it up after Sonya says "Don't touch me you filthy rotten slimeball", cheek to cheek annnnnnd....ACTION!

(Murphy drops the script; kisses Sonya; a lingering kiss she accepts; then he slowly pulls away.)

Sonya: *(to the air)* Okaaaay....

Hector: CUUUUT. What the hell was that?

Sonya: He's improvising.

Hector: What about the script?

Murphy: You told me to improvise.

(Hector enters the scene)

Hector: WITH THE HAT I SAID IMPROVISE; WITH THE HAT.

Murphy: What's wrong with improvising?

Hector: What's wrong with improvising?

Sonya: *(to the air)* S'okay with me.

Hector: Lemme-tell-you, lemme-tell-you Mr. Murphy what's wrong with improvising.

Murphy: Tell me...

Hector: IT TAKES TALENT.

Murphy: Oh Yeah? Well so does DIRECTING.

Hector: GET 'IM-OUTAHERE.

Touch

(Blackout. Murphy and Sonya exit through the closet; lights up bedroom.)

Isabel: Hector?

(Hector broods, staring at us)

How'd the audition go?

Hector: How'd the audition go?

Isabel: Uh huh?

Hector: Nathan Lane is lookin' pretty good right now.

Isabel: Come to bed Hector...

Hector: LORENZO LAMAS. IF THEY WOULD GIVE ME THE MONEY I COULD GET LORENZO LAMAS.

Isabel: Come to bed Hector.

Hector: This is a frustrating business.

Isabel: Make love to me Hector.

Hector: I HATE THIS GODDAMN BUSINESS.

(Isabel opens the sheets inviting him)

Isabel: Fuck me Hector.

Hector: *(unbuttons his shirt)* I'm a good director; I'm a good, respected-mother-fuckin'-director so why the hassle, WHY THE FUCKIN' HASSLE?

Isabel: I want you inside me Hector.

Hector: *(removes his pants)* I, I've got to rethink myself...

Sonya: I want it now.

Hector: *(strips down)* First there should be an air about me; don't you think there should be an air Isa?

Isabel: An air, an odor, whatever.

Hector: A good director should have a spirit in his speech; I HAVE A SPIRIT.

Isabel: Yes, yes you have Hector...

Hector: A brooding genius off the set but faithful to the classics.

Isabel: That's you Hector, that's you...

Hector: My leading lady has to be very sexy in a silent kind of way with round, firm breasts, not too big, pressed gently against my chest...

Isabel: Tell me about Other Times Hector...

Hector: *(slips into bed)* Other Times....I will ignore her.

Isabel: Of course you will.

Hector: *(on top of her)* I will be outwardly shy but possessing an inner strength and emotion that women and men notice immediately...

Isabel: Irresistible...

Touch

Hector: Yet unapproachable.

Isabel: And your hair, YOUR HAIR....

(She is savaging his hair with her fingers)

Hector: Wet and combed back; Denzel Washington yet Erich
    von Stroheim in one package!

Isabel: Yes!

*(Hector has an orgasm; he freezes; then rolls over beside
    Isabel. A short silence.)*

Hector: Isa....?

Isabel: Yes Denzel...?

Hector: Was it as good for you as it was for me?

*(Isabel looks to us. It wasn't so good. Light change;
    Hector exits; a spot remains on Isabel as she swings
    outa bed; jerks a suitcase from under the bed, checks its
    contents.)*

Isabel: *(to us)* Hector made love the way he drove a car but with
    that last wet dream, I got him outa my system; this morning
    I'm catching an early flight to Bali but first I took a long,
    hot bath to cleanse myself of the brooding genius; the scent
    of a dead man is not something you want to take to Bali.

(Slams the suitcase. Sniffs the air)

Isabel: *(to us)* I took another bath; that's the way I am; and on the plane to Bali I slipped into the flying toilet and took a little cat-bath in the mirror; that's the way it was; Me and the cat baths in the little flying toilet; don't look in the mirror: Images of Murphy and Sonya in the mirror; don't look; too late; I kept seeing Murphy and Sonya in the mirror at thirty-thousand feet; the two of them, sweating, savoring, mooing, cowing, and licking each other; I couldn't escape it; it was like, like, like....

> *(Immediately Murphy and Sonya appear, two stools, Mi Cocina Restaurant; lights out on Isabel. This scene transition should be seamless.)*

SCENE...

Murphy: "Like making love to a dead man?"

Sonya: I didn't say that.

Murphy: Is THAT how it was?

Sonya: Not exactly.

Murphy: Well what exactly?

Sonya: Well...

Murphy: It was your idea; "Your place or mine?"

Sonya: "WITH PASSION" you said. HA.

Touch

Murphy: What about "All the Earth's sand to the moon one grain at a time?"

Sonya: It was something I felt.

Murphy: *(to us)* You meet someone, you connect; you begin to feel things you haven't felt in awhile; you decide to act on those feelings and...

Sonya: Maybe our expectations were too high.

Murphy: Maybe?

BOTH: *(to us)* WE MUST'VE BEEN OUT OF OUR MINDS.

Murphy: Whadawe do now?

Sonya: WE? You're on your own kid. I-AM-SO-STUPID. My, my first mistake with you was an obvious one; the Scriptures are very clear on sexual matters; "When making love, the WOMAN is always on top." BIG MISTAKE.

Murphy: (to us) Hindsight; I can handle this.

Sonya: Actually I think Hector's death freed me. *(to the air)* I'm not sure if I need men anymore.

Murphy: *(to us)* NOT SURE. Watch this...

Sonya...

Sonya: *(to the air)* I DON'T need men anymore.

Murphy: *(to us)* Women LOVE mythology; watch this...

Sonya, I've read in ancient times men and women were ONE.

Sonya: You don't believe that Greek Mythology SHIT do you?

Murphy: Of course not, I just thought....

Sonya: *(to us)* This man should not think.

Lemme guess...YOU THOUGHT men and women were ONE and spent their entire lives losing their hair and dignity in strange relationships, on miserable searches for their OTHER HALF?

(to us) fun.

Murphy: *(to us)* We said goodbye...

Sonya: *(to us)* We decided to be realistic about it.

Murphy: *(to us)* None of that cliché shit...

Sonya: Hey, we can still be friends.

Murphy: Okay.

(to us) I hate that shit.

Sonya: You don't need another friend do you Murphy?

Murphy: No.

Sonya: What you <u>need</u> is an acrobat, lover, mate, nurse, cook, housekeeper, mother, concubine...

Touch

Murphy: *(to us)* Isabel.

blackout

> *(Lights up bedroom; Murphy sits on the bed, facing audience.)*

SCENE...

Murphy: *(to us)* Isabel was still in Bali but I had kept a key.

The first day was casual; I, I walked around to Barnes & Noble, picked up a copy of "Dianetics" just outa curiosity; sat on Isabel's bed and read for awhile; threw-up several times; had a cup of hot tea with lemon and honey; looked out the window for awhile; wound-up debating a pigeon on the window-sill about whether Marlin Perkins on Wild Kingdom was gay or not....I thought he was...she'll be back.

On the second day I decided to have some fun; I took a chance and dropped by the Equity Building; ran into Nathan Lane in the lobby; told him I hated his guts; he yelled for a policeman; I walked away... She'll be back.

Third day: I did one of those radio readings from famous novels at the Symphony Space; spoke to Jane Curtin a few minutes afterwards then came back here and waited....she'll be back.

Fourth day: Delivered a new headshot to my agent Alec; his door was bolted; a notice taped to the door read, "Property Seized by Order of the Bureau of Narcotics." Alec?

I wasn't feeling well after that so I stopped at one of those Korean delis and bought an orange; ONE DOLLAR FOR A LOUSY ORANGE. As I was leaving I ACCIDENTLY kicked a hole in a watermelon; the Korean manager ran after me screaming, "I SUE YOU, I SUE YOU." She'll be back.

Fifth day: I bought a box of <u>spaghetti</u> and thought of Sonya all day... she'll be back.

Sixth day: A friend invited me to a screening of THE LOCAL STIGMATIC, a film made from a play by Heathcote Williams; Al Pacino had made the film of the play and was showing it to a group representing the Berlin Film Festival. I went. Al was gracious; gave a short speech, then disappeared; the Berlin Group loved the film! "Savage, chilling, brilliantly funny!" they said. But there was very little talk of the film; THE TALK was about the playwright; it seems that after writing the play, Heathcote Williams had simply vanished. This was the late sixties I guess; for twenty odd years he had become an eccentric; one novel, a poem about whales, a book on dolphins, another on elephants; when last heard from he had taken up residence in a borrowed treehouse on some noble estate in Cornwall..... ROLE MODEL. That day I adopted Heathcote Williams.....She'll be back.

Touch

The Seventh Day was like shooting rubber bands at the moon; I didn't bathe, shave, brush my teeth or wash my face; I thought I'd gift-wrap the spaghetti and send it to Sonya to remember me; I ran to the kitchen to get the spaghetti; picked my orange from the bowl in the hallway; wrapped the orange to Sonya who should've gotten the spaghetti; tried to peel the spaghetti for myself who should've gotten the orange.... I'm delirious at this point; I hear a peck on the window; I look to the window...pigeon friend is laughing at me, other pigeons gather, anarchy was in the air; I ended the seventh day a frightened piece of meat on the floor in a corner of the bedroom watching Hitchock's "The Birds" being filmed outside my window.... She's not coming back; she's not coming back; she's not coming back.

blackout

(Music of doom fills the air.)
SCENE...

(Music down....lights up bedroom. Two weeks later; Isabel enters with a suitcase; steps on uncooked spaghetti.)

Isabel: What-tha...?

(she notices a note on the bed. Reads.)

Isabel: "Death, it is so quick, Murphy." *(thinks)* Huh....

(tosses the note; unpacks. stops)

161

Isabel: No; forget it.

(unpacks; stops)

Isabel: Murphy? Death? *(pause)* Ridiculous.

(continues unpacking)

Isabel: *(to us)* I mean, this is a man who rescues an injured pigeon on the street.

Okay Isabel, make yourself feel better. Call him. Ask him "Why the spaghetti on my floor?"

(to us) "Disconnected." I called his service; "We don't carry him anymore." His agent's door..."Narcotics seizure." Something's wrong. Do I exaggerate? Of course. That's the way I am; what am I suppose to do, call everyone he knew like some hysterical relative?

(telephone rings. Sonya appears on a stool, Mi Cocina Restaurant, holding an orange. Blackout bedroom; lights up restaurant.)

Sonya: (to us) She called. Sounded like some hysterical relative; I mean, what am I gonna say to this woman?

(Isabel joins her)

Isabel: I'm sorry I'm late.

Sonya: Oh that's okay....

(to us) I lied.

Touch

(Isabel cautiously sits on the stool.)

Isabel: I, I know ME-CALLING-YOU seems odd but....

(They examine each other; uncomfortable pause.)

Sonya: You don't look so perfect; he said....

Isabel: He said you were "Far from perfect."

Sonya: Do you really read "Dianetics" while smearing yourself with avocado and yogurt?

Isabel: I <u>do</u> but there's no connection; are you connecting?

Sonya: Yes.

Isabel: Then you should stop.

Sonya: I'll think about it.

Isabel: Anyway, I threw Dianetics into the ocean off the coast of Bali.

Sonya: Did it float?

Isabel: No.

Sonya: Of course it didn't; so, why did you call?

Isabel: Murphy's note.

Sonya: Read it again....

Isabel: *(reads)* "Death, it is so quick...Murphy."

Sonya: Miss Taiwan.

Isabel: 'Cuse me?

Sonya: Long story. He wanted us to know that.

Isabel: Know what?

Sonya: He's trying to scare you.

Isabel: That's not like him.

Sonya: He's a man.

Isabel: What about the spaghetti on the floor?

Sonya: He sent me an orange.

Isabel: An orange?

Sonya: Gift wrapped.

Isabel: Murphy would never give away an orange.

Sonya: Wanna bet? (reads a note) "A gift to remember me; I found it savage, chilling, and brilliantly funny..."

Isabel: An orange?

Sonya: "Love, Murphy."

Isabel: So strange...

Sonya: Isabel, all he's doing is transferring intimacy he can't deliver to another human; giving it to an orange is safer.

Isabel: No, something's wrong; something's WRONG.

Sonya: He wants you to think that.

Isabel: He has a full life, doesn't he? I mean, he's not depending on <u>us</u> is he?

Sonya: *(to us)* I'll try to put this delicately...OF COURSE HE'S DEPENDING ON US.

Isabel: His parents died in a train crash you know.

Sonya: *(to us)* She fell for the train-crash-story, I don't believe it...

Isabel: Coming home from skiing...

Sonya: Stratton?

Isabel: Sugarloaf.

Sonya: He told me Stratton...

Isabel: I'm telling you, he has NO-ONE.

Sonya: He has friends.

Isabel: He didn't have friends; I mean, he knew people, people in the biz but..

.Sonya: *(to us)* She's building up to something...

Isabel: I think he's dead.

Sonya: Oh come on....

ty adams

Isabel: Well what does a man do after receiving blow after blow after blow?

Sonya: *(to us)* What we ALL do; suck the bullet outa your arm and walk on down the street.

I don't know; what does a man do Isabel?

Isabel: He leaves a suicide note.

Sonya: Let me tell ya about suicide notes...I had this friend, a beautiful black woman, Odessa; she worked for an escort service; a daily regular of hers was a Hasid; fiftyish; he lies, he lies on a bed and Odessa, fully clothed, wearing a pair of pink, he-had-to-have-pink, <u>galoshes</u>; she jumps around the room like a child avoiding puddles....<u>guaranteed orgasm</u> within ten minutes!

Isabel: I don't believe that.

Sonya: Ten minutes. She eventually quit the service but he hounded her; sent her APOCALYPTIC NOTES; notes of death; he would kill himself if she didn't see him again. She didn't. He didn't. He found another puddle jumper; he's still alive, only ten minutes a day but still......

Isabel: Men are so fucked up.

Sonya: *(to us)* FINALLY...

Isabel: Don't you think so...?

Sonya: Oh I wouldn't go that far.

166

Touch

Isabel: And they pretend to be so fragile and raw...

Sonya: Raw spaghetti...

Isabel: On my floor; he could've cooked it but nooo; hoping I'd
    see it as a metaphor for his feelings, raw and exposed and
    I'd step on those feelings and break them.

Sonya: You did.

Isabel: Well...

Sonya: Pure deception on his part; designed to make you worry.

Isabel: It's not going to work.

Sonya: *(to us)* This kid is coming along.

    He's not dead Isabel.

Isabel: Then where is he?

Sonya: No. The question is WHO IS HE? He doesn't know so
    he hits bottom; leaves a note and goes on a search...

Isabel: A search for himself. I've read that. Actors do that.

Sonya: He's asking himself: Am I an actor? A taxi driver? A
    psychologist? Fruit activist? A man who deeply loves jazz
    or is Sonny Rollins simply an escape? A Renaissance man
    or merely a dogmatic flea?

Isabel: Could you run those past me again...

Sonya: He's in-flight. Men are in-flight Isabel. Women don't need them to buy fur coats anymore; oh, which reminds me...here's a NO FUR button.

(Sonya pins an activist button on Isabel)

Isabel: Does this mean I have to get rid of my mother's rabbit ear muffs?

Sonya: Yes; I'll bet you Murphy is safely wrapped in the cloak of Western Catskill Zen; sitting in the mountains somewhere eating curried lamb with some former arms-dealer-turned-bearded-guru in the back seat of a rented Rolls Royce.

(Sonya finishes pinning the button)

Sonya: There!

Isabel: I'd feel better if I knew where he was.

Sonya: Isabel honey, you and I, WOMEN need to know one thing...whom we're making love to; men are terrified of knowing who they really are...CATCH 22!

Isabel: CATCH 22?

(to us) I've been reading the wrong book.

Sonya: What you need my dear is The Craft of the Goddess.

Isabel: Salad-dressing?

Sonya: God-as-woman.

Isabel: Wow.

Touch

Sonya: *(seductive)* I will teach you THE CRAFT.

Isabel: Will it float?

Sonya: It'll float.

Isabel: What about Murphy?

Sonya: Murphy who?

Isabel: His parents weren't really killed in a train crash were they?

Sonya: No.

Isabel: He lied?

Sonya: Yes...

Isabel: But not about you.

Sonya: Nor you.

Isabel: You DO have alabaster skin...

Sonya: And YOU are perfect.

BOTH: I hate you.

Sonya: *(seductive)* I will teach you THE CRAFT. It will feel like a jolt from a state of murky existence; your mind will snap to attention; a shock of our beautiful hair will go flying from your head and tiny lightning bolts will appear in your eyes.

Isabel: I'm afraid of lightning.

(Sonya holds up the orange)

Sonya: It begins with <u>touch</u>...

(Sonya offers the orange)

Go on...

(Isabel touches)

Sonya: Take it....

(Isabel takes the orange)

Sonya: Touch redefines everything; hold it in your hands; turn it around; feel it; feel the shape, the size, the weight, the texture; the navel; notice the color, the reflection of light on its skin; bring it to your nose and smell it; bite into it, go ahead bite it; taste it; hear the sound as your teeth sink in; eat it; eat the orange; feel it slide down your throat; see it grow smaller in your hand; feel it grow larger in your belly; yes...eat it, eat it; feel its weight disappear in your hand; smaller, smaller; now, now when you've eaten it down to the smallest piece....let it disappear. Poof. Nothing. But you have it! You-have-that-orange! You've captured it; felt it; seen it; tasted it with your inner senses; and no one can take it away from you; you will never forget that orange....

(Sonya takes a napkin and wipes several bits of orange from Isabel's face.)

Sonya: It's there.....and there, and there, and there.

Touch

(They are close, a look)

(They kiss.)

blackout

SCENE...

(Lights up log cabin; the Catskill Mts.; Murphy drops his skiis, backpack, and a rolled-sleeping bag.)

Murphy: Sanctuary.

(He tries to read a brochure)

Let's see uhhh... *(reads)* "Adventure doesn't have to be far from home..." bla, bla, blaaa; "ZOAR OUTDOOR, located in the unspoiled Catskill Mountains offers whitewater rafting..."

Murphy: *(to us)* I like whitewater rafting...uhhh

(reads) "canoeing, rock climbing and ski touring with a base camp..."?

(to us) I didn't see a base camp.

(reads) "with a base camp and outfitters shop on the river, okay, ON THE RIVER. Uhhhh, "Zoar Outdoor, a division of WEST-CAT-ZEN, INC."

(to us) Parent company, that's good. Security.

(He tosses his sleeping bag)

(to us) I called, they said I could be a Whitewater-Rafting-Guide-Trainee; these cabins are only twelve bucks a night. Chopped firewood, two bucks a bundle; and in town, one mile away; here's the winner.... ORANGES, THREE FOR A DOLLAR.

(to the air) SOMEBODY STOP ME. I'm having too much fun.

(He stands, unpacks)

Murphy: *(to himself)* I'll get a bicycle; I LOVE BICYCLES; AND A DOG; I'LL GET A DOG...companionship.

(to us) I'm here to stay; It was a lot of things; not just that last miserable week; I, I'm sure Sonya ignored the orange and, and Isabel, she never reads notes; she'll simply think I spilled the spaghetti; no, it wasn't, wasn't that......

(thinks) There's an ancient Japanese love poem that goes: "Lying alone, my black hair tangled, uncombed, I long for the one who touched it first."

(to the air) This!

(to us) Oh I know what people will say; "That's corny. You'll miss the plays." I won't miss the plays......cold pizza; cell-phoning cab rides, shrieking car alarms, Korean deli managers, twenty-seven different coffee beans, I never used

more that six anyway and certainly not BLADING IN CENTRAL PARK.

(points to himself) <u>Bicycle.</u>

(to us) I won't miss....well, those shrimp dumplings from Ollie's at Broadway and Eighty-fourth but that's all I'll.....he makes them in the window; ancient chinese hip hop in the background, we stand on the street and applaud, he bows; it's better than front row seats at Carnegie Hall; oh Carnegie Hall; John's Pizza in the village; that huge flea market on twenty-sixth street; Au Truquet, little French restaurant in the west-vil; the Museum of Motion Pictures; a bottle of Napa Ridge Pinot Noir, room temp; oh yes, those free clay tennis courts that no one knows about; Sonny Rollins at the Beacon; Van Morrison at the Beacon; Cheryl Crow...

anybody at the Beacon; Cirque de Soleil; Shakespeare in the Park; Birdland; street fairs, Zabars, art galleries, WHAT THE HELL AM I DOING HERE?

(He begins packing with haste)

Murphy: Out of my mind, out of my mind, OUT OF MY FUCKING MIND.

(He straps the backpack on; jerks the closet door open; freezes; he is confronted with the image of Isabel, dressed in black leather, sort-of Emma Peel-meets-Mad Max look.)

Isabel: In-flight Murphy?

Murphy: Ohmigod...

Isabel: Going somewhere?

Murphy: Isabel? Is that you?

Isabel: Shut up Raft Boy.

Murphy: Raft boy?

Isabel: You left my apartment in a mess.

Murphy: I, I know, I know; I can explain...

Isabel: I don't care.

Murphy: No, no, no, it, it was, what it was...I needed a little distance that's all, but now I'm fine; I'm here and you're, you're....

Isabel: A woman on a mission.

Murphy: A-what?

Isabel: My new name is Star Hawk.

Murphy: That sounds familiar.

Isabel: Sonya gave it to me.

Murphy: And the hair under your arms?

Isabel: Growing.

Touch

Murphy: Really?

(Isabel raises her arm)

Isabel: Wanna touch?

Murphy: No thank you, I, I'm trying to quit.

Isabel: <u>Touch</u> is everything you know.

Murphy: Is it?

Isabel: Oh I want to thank you for the orange.

Murphy: That, that was....

Isabel: It was everything you described it to be.

Murphy: I was under a lot of stress that day Isabel...

Isabel: STAR HAWK.

Murphy: I'm sorry. What-do-you-want...<u>Star</u> <u>Hawk</u>?

Isabel: I WANT TO BE ON TOP.

Murphy: On top?

Isabel: I WANT TO TAKE A STAND: Pro-Choice; No Nukes; Save the Whales; the Rain Forests; Anti-Apartheid; break the chains, unleash the fury of women as a mighty force; find the answers to the big questions!

Murphy: I don't know what-tha-hell was bothering the serpent.

Isabel: Who gives a shit.

Murphy: A lot of religious people.

Isabel: I WANT TO BE ON TOP.

Murphy: Okay; I, I, I'm just having a little trouble dealing with the change.

Isabel: Deal-with-it.

Murphy: I remember "Humans-were-one-Isabel."

Isabel: WIMP.

Murphy: Wimp?

Isabel: Too perfect.

Murphy: Okay, okay, I, I said that, I did but...

Isabel: You're in-flight Murphy.

Murphy: I'm not in-flight.

Isabel: Men are in-flight.

Murphy: I WANT to be here Isabel.

Isabel: STAR HAWK.

Murphy: I'm sorry, I'm sorry, sorry.

Isabel: Women are changing Murphy.

Murphy: That's fine.

Isabel: Adapt.

Touch

Murphy: I've...

Isabel: ADAPT.

Murphy: I have adapted.

Isabel: This?

Murphy: I WANT TO BE HERE.

Isabel: Who are you Murphy?

Murphy: A WHITEWATER RAFTING GUIDE TRAINEE.

Isabel: (to the air) Ask a man who he is and he tells you what he
    does...

Murphy: WHITEWATER RAFTING...

Isabel: SHUT UP you little puddle-jumper.

Murphy: Puddle jumper?

Isabel: Who-are-you Murphy? Are you an actor? A psychologist
    drivin' a taxi? A man who deeply loves escape or is Sonny
    Rollins simply jazz to you? Or are you merely a dogmatic
    man with renaissance fleas?

Murphy: What?

Isabel: *(to us)* Oops, Fucked that one up.

Murphy: I know what you want.

Isabel: You tell me Murphy.

177

Murphy: I KNOOOW...what you want. But I'm not gonna do it. Not-going-to-do-it. I will not.

Isabel: You didn't get your bio-feedback-inducts cleaned out didya?

Murphy: NEVER.

Isabel: Wrong answer.

> *(Closet door slams. Murphy stands alone; looks to us; then cautiously opens the door; nothing; closes the door; sits on the floor, facing the audience; lights fade on an isolated, lonely figure.)*

Murphy: *(sings softly)* Just my imagination, runnin' away with me, It was JUST MY IMAGINAAATION, runnin' away with me......*(pause)* Smokey Robinson.

blackout

SCENE...

> *(A gong. Sobering oriental sound. Appearing in the space between the bedroom and two stools is a young woman, Japanese Tea Master Trainee Yoshi, wearing a kimono, split white socks, and an easy smile.*
>
> *The room is lighted with parchment sconces. Yoshi is carrying a tray with a bubbling black pot; two cups*

and napkins; and a wooden ladle spoon; Murphy goes to her, Yoshi bows.)

Yoshi: Welcome to Yoshi's Tatami Room.

(Murphy returns the bow)

Murphy: Thank you for seeing me on short notice.

Yoshi: What can I do for you Mr. Murphy?

Murphy: I WANT MY BIO-FEEDBACK INDUCTS CLEANED OUT.

Yoshi: (to us) There is no such thing as a bio-feedback induct.

Murphy: Will you do it?

Yoshi: Oki-doki.

(Yoshi sits, knees bent under; Murphy sits with knees bent under; Yoshi places the pot of tea on the floor and begins an arrangement; she then tends the kettle, ladling.)

Murphy: I can't believe you have a location in the mountains.

Yoshi: Hay Fever Branch.

Murphy: I'm early 'cause I'm, I'm a little nervous.

Yoshi: In Japan we say, "the early bird gets the fugu."

Murphy: The fugu?

Yoshi: A fish Mr. Murphy.

Murphy: I thought this was a tea room?

Yoshi: It is a tea room.

Murphy: And you're the tea master?

Yoshi: My father, The Master is away today.

Murphy: Who are you?

Yoshi: Tea Master Trainee.

Murphy: Trainee?

Yoshi: Humble trainee.

Murphy: I'm feeling a little uneasy.

Yoshi: On the phone you sounded desperate.

Murphy: I AM desperate.

Yoshi: Desperate-man cannot be choosy.

Murphy: *(to us)* This does not feel good.

> *(Yoshi tends the kettle, ladling four times, then stiffens, looks to the sky and closes her eyes.)*

Yoshi: The kettle is singing Mr. Murphy.

> *(to us)* To the untrained ear, of course, it is the sound of water boiling.

Murphy: What is that sound?

Touch

Yoshi: The kettle is singing.

Murphy: I hear water boiling.

Yoshi: We find peacefulness through the singing kettle; a bowl
of tea is spiritual, artistic, social, and...

(to us) It is delicious.

Murphy: But will it clean out my bio-feedback inducts?

Yoshi: *(ladles the tea)* You must be patient Mr. Murphy; you seek
peace; listen to the kettle sing; it is the sound of
enlightenment; the sound of wind chasing through the pine
forest...

(Murphy listens)

Murphy: If you think it'll help, I know a little Japanese poetry...

Yoshi: *(to us)* I hate Japanese poetry.

That will not be necessary Mr. Murphy...

Murphy: Okay...

Yoshi: Teaism is essentially a worship of the imperfect...

Murphy: I feel right at home.

Yoshi: *(to the air)* The kettle is singing.

Murphy: (to us) Finally a tender, sensuous woman; "the kettle is
singing" woman who worships the imperfect; god knows
what she could do for my family.

Yoshi: Can you hear it singing Mr. Murphy?

Murphy: Not really. Do you think I'm a dogmatic man with Renaissance fleas?

Yoshi: Not for me to say.

Murphy: Tell me, is it possible to have too much FUN?

Yoshi: *(to us)* That depends on what you put in your tea.

Murphy: My parents thought so.

Yoshi: Your parents forgot history lesson Mr. Murphy...

(to us) It wasn't called the Boston Tea Party for nothing.

(Yoshi pours a cup of tea.)

Yoshi: We are ready Mr. Murphy; with this you will forget the rest of the world.

(Murphy grabs tea cup; Yoshi stops him.)

Yoshi: No, no, no. First make sure your napkin is folded on the diagonal with the point creased up; upper body bent at the waist; then ladle your tea with four fingers pointing straight; two hands; you must use two hands, tea cup cradled; long sips; one at a time.

(Murphy follows instructions; takes a long sip.)

Yoshi: In order to find your way, you must become primitive, meditate and forget...that is the way of tea.

Touch

(Murphy has finished drinking a long sip; pulls the cup down.)

Yoshi: Let the devils out, the happiness in.

(Murphy looks inside the empty cup.)

Murphy: There's something in the bottom.

Yoshi: Of course.

Murphy: Is it important?

Yoshi: Not really.

Murphy: I think it is. There's this woman on Amsterdam Avenue., Sister Rev. Cherokee, she reads tea leaves...this is important.

Yoshi: That's not the way of tea Mr. Murphy.

Murphy: Yeah, well "The-way-of-tea" might be overlooking something.

Yoshi: For one thousand years Mr. Murphy...

Murphy: I just thought...

Yoshi: THOUGHT will cripple you Mr. Murphy. This tea thing, it is a small thing, perhaps we reveal ourselves too much in small things because we have so little of the great to conceal.

(to us) My high school thesis paper...

Murphy: Listen, I've, I've got twelve kids waiting in a raft to go screaming down a river; it is not a <u>small</u> <u>thing</u> if I'm late; so can we...

Yoshi: You must be patient Mr. Murphy.

(to us) stupid man; go to Barnes and Noble and buy the Book.

Murphy: By any chance, is there a <u>book on tea</u>...?

Yoshi: No.

Murphy: *(to us)* I'm not gonna beg this woman for answers; I'm not gonna do it...

(pause; offers his cup, begs) Pleeeeze help me; I need answers; pleeeeze....

Yoshi: The way of tea is not to give answers Mr. Murphy.

Murphy: Then what-tha-hell am I doing here?

Yoshi: *(explodes)* take your shit to Sister Rev. Cherokee.

(to us) oops...

Murphy: You should take some time off Yoshi.

Yoshi: My apology Mr. Murphy.

Murphy: Whitewater rafting helps.

Yoshi: Perhaps I was a little...

(to us) <u>fed up</u>.

Murphy: Now, can we...?

Yoshi: You want answers?

Murphy: Yes.

Yoshi: You want the <u>Lunch</u> <u>Special</u>.

Murphy: The lunch special? What's that?

Yoshi: Give me ten dollars.

Murphy: Ten dollars?

Yoshi: Gimme.

> *(Murphy digs out a ten dollar bill, hands it to her, she takes it, pockets it. Yoshi briefly glances at the bottom of the tea cup.)*

Murphy: Okay now we're getting somewhere. What? What is it?

Yoshi: I see a woman.

Murphy: Is she wearing black leather?

Yoshi: She's wearing a lot of sadness.

Murphy: Isabel. She misses me. Okay, what else?

Yoshi: She's having a lot of difficulty with men.

Murphy: Other men. Uh huh. Go on, go on, go on...

185

Yoshi: She's not enjoying her life.

Murphy: She wants to be on top. She can be on top; she can...what?

Yoshi: All her life she has followed men.

Murphy: Isabel?

Yoshi : The woman must make a change.

Murphy: She did. Changed her name to Star Hawk.

Yoshi: The woman must do it now.

Excuse me, 'cuse me, 'cuse me.

(Yoshi stands, walks)

Murphy: Okay, bathroom break. Right? you'll be right back, right?

(Murphy looks at his watch...as scones dim. He's alone.)

(Gong)

blackout.

SCENE...

(The sound of leaves rustled by the wind; a sense of season's changing; lights up Isabel's bedroom, two months later; Isabel is busy packing two dozen oranges. telephone rings; Murphy appears, Mi Cocina Restaurant;

Touch

both speak straight ahead to the air during the phone call.)

Isabel: Hello?

Murphy: Isabel?

Isabel: Speaking.

Murphy: It's, it's Murphy.

Isabel: Murphy?

Murphy: Yeah, it's me.

Isabel: Murphy, I don't believe it; where are you?

Murphy: I'm in town for a few days; you know, supplies; trade a few pelts.

Isabel: Sooo, you DID go to the mountains.

Murphy: Oh yeah; actually I'm here to catch a movie; go by Equity, you know, check out the biz.

Isabel: Ohhh god; this, this is so....unexpected.

BOTH: How've you been?

Murphy: You first.

> *(Isabel looks to the bed; someone is asleep under the sheets.)*

Isabel: Well, life's good...different.

Murphy: Different? How?

(Isabel glances again at the bed)

Isabel: Different.

Murphy: I dreamt about you; you had changed your name to Star Hawk.

Isabel: It's already taken.

Murphy: I know.

Isabel: Murphy, are you okay?

Murphy: Me? Fine; I'm in the mountains now.

Isabel: Right; you said that.

Murphy: Yeah...

Isabel: Eating curried lamb...

Murphy: Oranges...

Isabel: Oh I LOVE ORANGES!

Murphy: You hated oranges...

Isabel: I was outa touch back then; remember that biofeedback induct stuff.

Murphy: *(to us)* YOSHI EVERY WEDNESDAY, I love it.

Isabel: I'm SO GLAD you didn't buy into that crap... *(pause)* Murphy?

Murphy: Yeah me, me too....

Isabel: I've thought about you; riding around in a Rolls Royce; practicing Zen....

Murphy: No, no, no, just me and my dog.

Isabel: You have a dog?

Murphy: Yeah...

Isabel: I want a dog.

Murphy: Heathcoat.

Isabel: Heathcoat...

   (to us) Naming your dog after a British airport?

Murphy: A lot of people think of Heathrow; the British airport.

Isabel: Stupid people.

Murphy: Really.

Isabel: Nice name, Heathcoat.

Murphy: Yeah...I left him with a dog sitter.

Isabel: Oh.

Murphy: Dog sitters are expensive.

Isabel: They are.

Murphy: Listen, I wanted to explain that note I left in your apartment.

Isabel: No, no, no...

Murphy: And, and the spaghetti...

Isabel: Oh that's okay; understood.

Murphy: Stupid.

Isabel: No.

Murphy: Yes.

Isabel: You were under a lot of stress that week.

Murphy: I was, I was under...

Isabel: A LOT...

Murphy: (pause) Isabel...?

Isabel: Yes?

Murphy: Are we, are we connecting?

Isabel: Connecting? I, I don't know...

Murphy: I think we are.

Isabel: I, I guess we are.

Murphy: WE ARE...

Isabel: Well, whadaknow.

Touch

Touch

Murphy: I mean we never did in the past so It feels, it feels...

Isabel: Good.

Murphy: It does...

Isabel: Well, a little distance...

Murphy: Helps.

Isabel: It does.

Murphy: Yeah...

Isabel: Murphy, did you find what you were looking for in the mountains?

Murphy: Imperfection? Misery? Loneliness? Yeah, I'd say I have; sure.

Isabel: That's good; 'cause you were pretty...

Murphy: Unhappy, I know.

Isabel: You didn't know who you were did you? *(pause)* Murphy?

Murphy: Does anybody?

(Isabel looks to the bed)

Isabel: Some people do.

Murphy: Then I hate those people.

Isabel: You're not "having too much fun" in those mountains are you? Remember, "too much..." ?

Murphy: No. Yes, I remember; no, I'm not having, no...but I'm trying; when that raft hits those rapids on the Esopus and those kids; the laughter; hysterical-crying-laughter; well, it's, it's fun...

Isabel: That's great; Adirondack Wildwaters?

Murphy: No. Zoar Outdoor.

Isabel: Zoar?

Murphy: Yeah...

Isabel: I do uhhh..

Murphy: Adirondacks.

Isabel: Right.

Murphy: That's okay; uhhh Adirondack's...good, good mountain.

Isabel: I suppose so....

BOTH: (pause) Well, I...

Isabel: This feels sooo good.

Murphy: Yeah; I think about you.

Isabel: I, I'm not perfect anymore.

Murphy: I don't know why I said that.

Isabel: Because I was out-of-touch.

Murphy: I don't know about that.

Isabel: Oh I heard about your agent.

Murphy: Alec...?

Isabel: Yeah...is he...?

Murphy: Okay? Yeah, probation; community service; I heard he stole away to Calcutta for awhile; tried to find himself; came back; broke his leg...

Isabel: Broke his leg...?

Murphy: chasing some guy down Ninth Avenue...

Isabel: Why?

Murphy: Trying to get his wallet back.

Isabel: Death wish.

Murphy: For a thin piece of fake leather with nothing in it.

Isabel: People like that...

Murphy: Who needs espresso...

Isabel: Really...

Murphy: Then he got his <u>leg</u> <u>cast</u> caught in a subway door.

Isabel: Oh no...

Murphy: Reached down and dropped his glasses on the tracks.

Isabel: Don't tell me...

Murphy: No, he let the glasses go....

Isabel: Oh that's good.

Murphy: I heard he's been hangin' out at Barnes & Noble...

Isabel: Oh I love that place.

Murphy: Addiction/Recovery Section.

Isabel: Second floor.

Murphy: Right...

Isabel: My favorite shelf is labeled "Anger and Stress."

Murphy: Well you might bump into him.

Isabel: Is he okay?

Murphy: Oh yeah, he's safe now....he's in <u>advertising</u>.

Isabel: That's good.

Murphy: I thought about Sonya the other day.

Isabel: Did you?

Murphy: I was eating spaghetti.

Isabel: I took flowers out to Hector's grave.

Murphy: <u>Yellow</u> flowers?

Touch

Isabel: White...that's good, yellow; no...white tulips for little Hec.

Murphy: Lemme-tell-you, lemme-tell-you..."

Isabel: "Damn-good-director..."

Murphy: Hector.

Isabel: Yeah....

Murphy: He's dead.

Isabel: Makes ya wonder...

Murphy: It does...

Isabel: Yeah...Listen, I, I've gotta shoot...

Murphy: Mexico?

Isabel: Bermuda.

Murphy: Ever do any shoots in the Catskills?

Isabel: No.

Murphy: I'll let you go.

Isabel: Okay.

Murphy: No...I need to see you.

Isabel: I'd love to but...

(Sonya from under the sheets)

Sonya: ISABEL? Isabel, are you talkin' to me?

Isabel: No.

Murphy: Who was that?

Isabel: Nobody.

Sonya: Isabel...?

Isabel: Shhhh....

Murphy: Who was that?

Isabel: My, my....I live with someone.

Murphy: Oh.

Isabel: It's, it's, it's...

Murphy: It'd be so good to see you.

Isabel: I have to go now....

Murphy: Meet me.

Isabel: I, I can't..

Murphy: Anywhere.

Isabel: I can't.

Murphy: Macy's is having a sale.

Isabel: Macy's is <u>always</u> having a sale.

Murphy: I need winter shirts; you know, in the mountains.

Isabel: Flannel?

Murphy: Right.

Isabel: First floor.

Murphy: Meet me there... *(pause)* meet me...

Isabel: I, I can't do this.

Murphy: I'm sorry.

Isabel: Take care.

Murphy: You too.

    (BLACKOUT Murphy. Sonya sits up in the bed)

Sonya: Isabel?

Isabel: Yes?

Sonya: Who was that?

Isabel: Oh, uhhh....work. Go back to sleep.

Sonya: That's easy...

    (Sonya disappears under pillow)

Sonya: Are you in-flight today?

Isabel: In-flight?

Sonya: That shoot in Bermuda? Remember?

Isabel: Yeah.....

Sonya: Well...?

(Isabel opens closet, rummaging)

Isabel: I am in-flight.

Sonya: How long?

Isabel: I don't know.

Sonya: *(rises in bed)* You always know.

Isabel: I'll call you; go back to sleep.

Sonya: What are you looking for?

(Isabel shakes out a flannel shirt.)

Isabel: Flannel.

Sonya: Mine.

Isabel: I know....I need it.

Sonya: You NEED FLANNEL?

Isabel: Uh huh.

Sonya: In Bermuda?

Isabel: I may get cold.

(Isabel holds the flannel shirt to her cheek.)

Sonya: I don't want you to get cold.

Isabel: I may miss you.

Touch

Sonya: I want you to miss me.

Isabel: But I'll need this.

Sonya: Take it.

Isabel: Thanks...

> *(Sonya slips under the sheets again; Isabel packs the flannel; closes the suitcase.)*

Isabel: Water my plants?

> *(From under the sheet an arm extends; Sonya reaching out; her finger extended. Their fingers touch. Isabel walks to exit. Stops. Looks back. Exits.)*

end of play

Made in the USA